# VOODOO EXCESS

Jeremy Reed

# VOODOO EXCESS

ENITHARMON PRESS

*To John Robinson, Mark Jackson and
Kevin Tierney with love*

First published in 2015
by Enitharmon Press
10 Bury Place
London WC1A 2JL

www.enitharmon.co.uk

Distributed in the UK by
Central Books
99 Wallis Road
London E9 5LN

Distributed in the USA and Canada by
Independent Publishers Group
814 North Franklin Street
Chicago, IL 60610
USA
www.ipgbook.com

Text © Jeremy Reed 2015
Introduction © R.J. Dent 2015

ISBN: 978-1-907587-50-4

Enitharmon Press gratefully acknowledges the financial support of
Arts Council England, through Grants for the Arts.

Individuals contribute to sustain the Press through the
Enitharmon Friends Scheme. We are deeply grateful to all Friends,
particularly our Patrons: Colin Beer, Sean O'Connor and those
who wished to remain anonymous.

British Library Cataloguing-in-Publication Data.
A catalogue record for this book is available
from the British Library.

Designed in Albertina by Libanus Press
and printed in England by
Short Run Press

# CONTENTS

*Introduction: The Rolling Stones and Jeremy Reed*     9

## PART 1 – THE GREATEST ROCK AND ROLL BAND IN THE WORLD

| | |
|---|---|
| Jumping Jack Flash | 15 |
| Keith Richards | 17 |
| Solid Bass – Bill Wyman | 18 |
| Charlie Watts | 20 |
| Brian Jones | 21 |
| Mick Taylor (Blues Avatar) | 22 |
| Ronnie Wood | 23 |

## PART 2 – THE BRIAN JONES YEARS: 1962–1969

| | |
|---|---|
| *The Stones at the Scene (1)* | 27 |
| Crawdaddy 1963 | 30 |
| Edith Grove | 32 |
| Andrew Loog Oldham | 34 |
| Regent Sound | 36 |
| Chess Studio 1964 | 38 |
| *The Stones at the Scene (2)* | 40 |
| American Tour 1964 | 42 |
| Kicking in 1964 | 44 |
| Burn | 45 |
| Marianne Faithfull (1) | 47 |
| The Last Time | 49 |
| *The Stones at the Scene (3)* | 50 |
| Brian's Off the Wall | 53 |
| Play With Fire | 54 |

| | |
|---|---:|
| Aftermath | 55 |
| Sun Going Down (On Me) | 57 |
| Courtfield Road | 59 |
| *The Stones at the Scene (4)* | 61 |
| Paint It Black | 64 |
| Moroccan Interlude | 66 |
| Hotel Minzah | 68 |
| Keith Richards 1967 | 70 |
| The Rolling Stones' Aesthetic | 72 |
| Keith Richards' Rhythm Trick | 74 |
| Neronian | 76 |
| Wormwood Scrubs | 78 |
| Brixton Prison | 79 |
| Hang Fire (Europe 1967) | 81 |
| The Rolling Stones Live | 83 |
| Brian Jones Trips | 85 |
| Satanic Advocates | 87 |
| Their Satanic Majesties Request | 89 |
| Skewed | 90 |
| Crossfire Hurricane | 92 |
| Beggars Banquet | 94 |
| Olympic Studios (Left on the Floor) | 95 |
| Going Down | 97 |
| Marianne Faithful (2) | 99 |
| Street Fighting Man | 100 |
| The Rock & Roll Circus | 102 |
| Breaking Up is Hard to Do | 104 |
| The Big Splash | 105 |
| Memo from Turner | 107 |
| Death by Water – Brian Jones | 109 |

## PART 3 — THE MICK TAYLOR YEARS: 1969–74

| | |
|---|---:|
| Mick Taylor | 113 |
| Winter | 114 |
| Rehearsals | 116 |
| The Stones in the Park | 117 |
| Sugar and Spice | 119 |
| Hyde Park 5 July 1969 | 121 |
| Miami 1969 | 125 |
| Roll Call (1969) | 127 |
| The L.A. Forum '69 | 129 |
| Bowing Out | 130 |
| Jagger's Dance Steps | 132 |
| Nasty Habits: Mick Taylor's Rolling Stones | 134 |
| Satan Rising (Altamont 1969) | 142 |
| Myth | 145 |
| Death | 147 |
| Saturnalia (1970) | 149 |
| Sticky Fingers | 152 |
| Farewell Tour 1971 | 153 |
| About Face | 154 |
| Tropical Disease | 156 |
| Tropical Diseases a.k.a. Exile on Main Street | 158 |
| Villefranche | 164 |
| Cocksucker Blues | 165 |
| Ladies and Gentlemen | 166 |
| Byron and Jagger | 167 |
| The Big Freeze | 169 |
| Goat's Head Soup | 171 |

## PART 4 – MEMORABILIA/BONUS MATERIAL

| | |
|---|---|
| Buying Stones Bootlegs at the Stables | 177 |
| Ham Yard W1 | 179 |
| Tongue and Lip | 183 |
| Pop Slice | 184 |
| Cops and Robbers | 185 |
| Mick Jagger's Lipsticks 1972–1978 | 186 |
| Performance | 187 |

## PART 5 – THE RONNIE WOOD YEARS: 1975–

| | |
|---|---|
| The Rolling Stones | 191 |
| A Difference of Cigarette Angles (Keith and Ronnie) | 193 |
| Stones Gene | 195 |
| Seventies | 196 |
| Some Girls | 198 |
| Disreputable | 202 |
| Longevity | 203 |
| Jack and Ginger | 204 |
| Mismanaged Striptease | 205 |
| Indestructible | 206 |
| Voodoo Hoodoo | 207 |
| 40 Licks (Backstage) | 208 |
| A Bigger Bang | 209 |
| Twickenham | 210 |
| Review | 211 |
| Drift Away | 212 |
| Why the Rolling Stones Are So Skinny | 213 |
| Bang | 214 |
| Later | 215 |
| Black as a Limo's Black | 216 |
| Swamp Blues | 217 |
| Stones 50 | 219 |

# Introduction:
## The Rolling Stones and Jeremy Reed

R J DENT

The Rolling Stones are far more than just a rock and roll band. The band is a cultural behemoth; the individual members are rock gods. The band's music, exploits, concerts, drug busts, line-up changes, arrests, convictions, films, girlfriends, wives, addictions, fights, tours, hedonistic lifestyles and out-and-out rebellion are the stuff of larger-than-life legend and rock and roll folklore. As members of the Rolling Stones, Mick, Keith, Ronnie and Charlie have lived incredible lives and have continued making music for half a century. They have also caused controversy, made some wonderful music, and seemingly defied medical science.

In Mick Jagger and Keith Richards, the band has a formidable focal point. No other frontman has the voice, the moves, the force, the appeal, the charisma, or the power of Mick Jagger. Keith Richards defies description; there is no adjective adequate enough to describe 'the human riff'. His guitar riffs are burned into the public's psyche. The opening chords of a Rolling Stones' song (*Start Me Up, Satisfaction, Honky Tonk Woman, Jumpin' Jack Flash*) are instantly, recognisably, memorably – and somehow indefinably – Keith riffs. The Glimmer Twins define the band – and there is no other band like the Rolling Stones.

Jeremy Reed is, by his own admission, obsessed with the Rolling Stones. For over twenty years he has written poems and essays and books about the rebellious outlaw 'King crows' of rock and roll. 'I like the Stones because of their image,' he says, partly explaining the obsession. 'They are the archetypal rebels.'

This book, *Voodoo Excess*, is the latest creative result of that ongoing obsession. And of course it's not just the image, but all aspects of the Rolling Stones that interest and obsess Jeremy Reed: from their music to their films; from their concert tours to their drug busts to their album covers to their mythology.

The Rolling Stones were first introduced as 'the greatest rock and roll band in the world' in 1969, and it is a title the band has retained for over four decades. For Reed, everything about the Rolling Stones as a musical and cultural phenomenon, and everything public and mythical, anecdotal and apocryphal about the larger-than-life individual band members, is simply the raw material that exists to be shaped into memorable lyric poetry.

In *Voodoo Excess*, Reed chronicles the band's progress from its early days at the Crawdaddy Club in 1962 to the fiftieth anniversary in 2012; he explicates Mick Jagger's dance steps and his accent; he examines the Rolling Stones' logo; and different ways Keith Richards and Ronnie Wood angle their cigarettes; he describes the emotional impact of the Stones' Hyde Park performance; he details the Redlands bust and the anti-establishment stance and attitude of the band; and he looks unflinchingly at the violence of Altamont and the inevitable death of the summer of love.

Individually, and as a band, the Rolling Stones are vividly brought to life in this collection. In *Voodoo Excess*, Reed shows us Mick Jagger's 'junglishly primal' stage persona; he presents Keith Richards as the band's 'wolfishly unkempt' ragged lieutenant; he reveals Brian Jones as 'the solitary deposed leader'; Bill Wyman as the 'ageless ... mainstay' of the band; and Charlie Watts as the 'percussion guru' the band relies upon for 'nailing down the sound'.

Showing fidelity to all line-ups of the legendary outlaw band, Reed paints detailed poetic portraits of the 'taciturn, undervalued' Mick Taylor and the 'stoned, clownish, tricky' Ronnie Wood. He also includes concise descriptions of select members of the Stones' entourage: their manager, the 'ex-Quant window dresser', Andrew Loog Oldham; Brian Jones's companion – the 'real' Anita Pallenberg; and that 'King's Road gamine', Marianne Faithfull.

Jeremy Reed also takes the reader of *Voodoo Excess* on a tour of the places that were crucial to the Stones' musical, visual and stylistic development: from the Crawdaddy Club (where they first performed as the Rolling Stones), Edith Grove, Cheyne Walk, the Scene Club in Ham Yard, and Courtfield Road, to Stargroves, Hyde Park, Twickenham, the L.A. Forum, and, finally, Altamont.

Throughout *Voodoo Excess*, Reed appropriates the names of several Rolling Stones' songs as titles to his poems. Sometimes he poetically deconstructs or reworks a particular song; sometimes he uses a song as a jumping-off point to a poem about a different Stones-related issue. The song titles that get reworked include: *Jumpin' Jack Flash, Let it Bleed, The Last Time, Play With Fire, Street Fighting Man, Gimme Shelter, Paint it Black* and *Sympathy For the Devil*. He also deconstructs and explicates the Stones' classic albums, including: *Aftermath, Their Satanic Majesties Request, Beggars Banquet, Exile on Main Street,* and *A Bigger Bang*.

*Voodoo Excess* is far more than a Rolling Stones biography and it is far more than a collection of Rolling Stones-themed poems and prose-poems – what Jeremy Reed has achieved with *Voodoo Excess* is to provide an incredibly in-depth, up-close and intimate chronicle of the life and times of a group of musicians who have – for fifty years – collectively and individually continued to define the term 'rock and roll rebels'.

# PART 1

# THE GREATEST ROCK AND ROLL BAND IN THE WORLD

## JUMPING JACK FLASH

He's a hoodo mambo
strutting a rumba
white Africana
junglishly primal
his undertones glottaly
South London, Dartford.
Cool in a tiara
or mink balaclava
he's made up and trashy
to strut it on boards
like a bashy pasha
or Berber bellydancer
his undertones glottaly
South London, Dartford.
He's a symbiotic
Diaghilev, Nureyev,
finger-wagging exorcist
mean-eyed mesmerist
coming on vatic
his undertones glottaly
South London, Dartford.
He's uncontestably
freeze-framed 1960s
gender-antagonist
bitchy svengali
swatch-tongued and counting
his riches like Dali
his undertones glottaly
South London, Dartford.
He's a voodoo instructor
who won't let you in
a class infiltrator
a snappy alligator

in-concert contortionist
raunchily prurient
but with a limp wrist.
He's a bluesy avatar
runway infanta
a right to the roots star
rock epic exponent
his undertones glottaly
South London, Dartford

## KEITH RICHARDS

So laid back, living where his dimension
touches on inner vision, that far gone
he wouldn't notice a black spotting fly
settle on a cheek and a second one

glint as a double beauty mark.
Heroin as an embalming fluid,
a cellular rejuvenator, he's
like Burroughs, a human experiment

in survival. Fortified, whiskey-shot,
the music lines are always tight, the nerves
feel into that non-committal control;
the man lives for the chords he generates,

and is a kind of latter day Crowley,
an adept of a deathless state, someone
who guards somatic knowledge, most alive
confronting stadia; knee boots, jewellery,

fetishistic tinctures of Joy,
hair brushed in every way that's contrary,
the archetypal rock star, maintaining
the image as reality

through so many mutations, Swiss clinics,
and in retreat at Redlands, someone who
finds a centre in the crazy decades.
'I'm dying, but that means I'm living too.'

## SOLID BASS — BILL WYMAN

He's triple c: Caroline, cavalier,
Charles II hairstyled,
deep-Englished

in propensities, eccentricities,
sunglassed, unaffected gecko
absorbing background naturally

and plotting mainstay chords
as though his bass is diaphragmed
as heartbeat to the song

auscultation
like hearing voices in a well
a deep down resonance.

He's chewing gum and high collars
Regency waistcoat coloured damson
his presence making inertia a style

of dispassionate statuary.
It's image, and he'll cook the girls
another hotel later,

get lipsticked like a horned bacchante
by the orgiastic.
Inscrutably no-give on stage

he's moated round, unreachable,
but there like foundations rooted
in an ivied manor.

He's ageless amongst 60s' youth,
Rolls-Royced and diaristic,
band-chronicler writing it down

like a rock-history Tacitus,
the crazies, riots, outrage on the road,
the sheer unprecedented worship.

## CHARLIE WATTS

The dandified time-instructor with sticks,
impeccable threads (ever see a cat
stay Ivy League mod 50 years
no flash, just seminally lived-in cool)
a style ripple up on a stool,
a bit Chinese, the partial sunken look,
face shaped like a grainy walnut
bashing the stack out for a two-hour drive
through blues licks tooled with angry torque
smack in the backbeat of 'Jumping Jack Flash'
like piloting a hurricane
through a compacted disused tube station.
We love him for his silence in the storm
his indomitable rhythm laid down
like a cheesed mogul whipping stakeholders.
Taciturn, underexposed, left of back
in the raw sonic tsunami, he leads
a broody Robert Johnson blues, brushes
tap-dancing palette on the skins, a slash
of magenta toned into peacock tints.
Nobody sees the drummer age, white shock
like a silver cactus tuft: a weapons devotee,
US vintage shooters, stick-up handguns;
percussion guru nailing down the sound
as heartbeat, a counter-rhythmic shuffle
under the tone-drop riff swishing like a switchblade.

## BRIAN JONES

So delicate an intrusion on noise,
a sitar, harpsichord, peacock's feather,
always the right tone in the melody,
a slide-guitar or dulcimer, blonde hair
shielding the eyes, no gender clue

offered in the lace blouse, mandarin coat,
jewellery picked up from Saks Fifth Avenue,
velvets from the Chelsea Antique Market.
Rejected, one way through is to mutate

to a new species, go away from life
and re-invent it, become solitary,
the only one looking out for others.
In time, the mutants, trans-people arrive
and infiltrate at festivals.
They are the enlightened ones, dressed in gold,

they live behind the hills or else nowhere.
It's a story of degeneration,
how drink and drugs get into overdrive
and how the fingers no longer find chords,

but tremble. It's the myth of dying young
recurs as a brutal reality.
Brian Jones face down in his swimming pool
murdered one sultry July night,
a ritual sacrifice to the sixties.

## MICK TAYLOR (BLUES AVATAR)

A bluesy drop-in out of nowhere
into Olympic sessions, riffy chromosomes
Mick Taylor, shy virtuoso maestro
Bluesbreakers apprentice interloper
tweaking romance into gutsy figures

like a decorative helium curve
a rainbow vaporizing in the song,
the adept androgynous enigma,
no pretensions, no working the stage lip
for provocation, but textured into

the sound like initializing a river
tracking from Barnes to the Mississippi,
a propulsive maverick avatar
coating rock licks with Taylor chemistry,
a country lesion, louche arpeggio,

its distinctive fingerprint's always right
like inventing new colours for a Pantone chart
through urgent messaging. He doesn't bond,
he's the supply player, the resources
pinching chords into acute bleeding grief

blue blood, not red, blocks of eloquent slide.
He's the introspective facility,
the guitar firm, but exoplanetary,
habituated pretty edge-walker
so modestly cool with heart-stopping slide

it's like liberating sonic chakras
on a guitar stem, blue morning glories
popping open inside 'Love In Vain,'
the fretwork, those filigree fingertips
sounding like sunshine floating through the rain.

## RONNIE WOOD

The impromptu interventionist slide-emperor
generic London blues his dialect
chord-wrangler stroking reconstructed BB King
into Stones aggro – he's all swoop and dodge
the nifty hipster rude boy front-man brat
doing the song with raw sexual chutzpah
like he'd knock a hyped-up scarlet Ferrari flat.
Ronnie's crow-profile snouts a cigarette
like it's a balance point, some extrasensory
fine-tuning to get balance right, a fag's
blue curly bootlace of drift-smoke. He's there
by default, euphoric obituarist
to Brian Jones, Mick Taylor, virtuoso blonds
dusting a genii's fingerprint on bottleneck
to make indigo arpeggios bleed.
Ronnie's a river bargee, born into the Thames
with boat-speak: water talks like a guitar
blurring boundaries between rhythm and lead
like late Stones meshing strutting back of Mick
and parallel to the resistant human riff's
brushstrokes that colour-code 'Gimme Shelter'
to dystopian flameout stormy blues.
He wears the look: a slept-in dandified rehab
persistence, odd Stone out, but majorly
textured into rock circus – see him run –
stoned, clownish, tricky with dexterity
patching the sound like he's hemming a coat.

# PART 2

# THE BRIAN JONES YEARS: 1962–1969

## THE STONES AT THE SCENE (1)

Grouped together in the warm Soho dark the fans could hear the raw, subversive hoot of Mick Jagger's harmonica, a lawless wail of self-taught anarchy, punctuating a maracas-driven revamp of Buddy Holly's `Not Fade Away', given all the insolent primitivism of sixties' R&B punk. There was no doubt that he was connecting with a streetwise London sound that had the edge on Motown, Ska and imported R&B; it was authentic Dartford, a South London swipe at Blues that had the audience ripping up the stage.

They turned up the heat on 'I Just Wanna Make Love To You', the singer's faux negroid inflexions no longer awkward, but squeezing the lyric like an orange, for the sticky crush of fangirls and fanboys grabbing at his neatly booted ankles. Jagger's toe-pivotal mince was generic stripper's routine, a striptease performed to the soundtrack of frenetic R&B, and mostly lost on a band still learning rhythmically to keep time.

The Stones played right on the audience, sweaty, punk, maladjusted and sneering, but were really middle class pretend street rats whose social revolution was confined to their intransigent, re-gendered facility to look like their music.

The Stones were bleeding what they did best, into a slow, broody, life-in-a-doorway, appealing Blues. Jagger announced it as one of theirs – 'Empty Heart' –and it was that – and the fangirls broke up at the contemptuously drawlish delivery, saturating the packed room; the seditious faggy tone in the voice, synonymous with the breakdown of gender identities in the ubiquitously de-masculinised times.

The Stones were killing the basement with their crude three-chord Rock banditry, like urban pirates playing way beyond noise limitation levels, doing 'Bye Bye Johnny' so fast it was like nothing ever played before.

The Stones audibly launched into a buccaneering, rocky 'Route 66', the guitars wrecked from playing too fast, the bass descending off-key, and the vocal so guttural, it was somehow the insurgent voice of rebellious youth right now, in a rundown Soho yard – Ronan O'Rahilly's pivotal Scene Club.

This time the Stones made the black painted walls of the club sweat with their raw, punkish frisson, so the Mod audience only had eyes for the draggy singer's contorted manipulation of green, red and yellow painted maracas on the Buddy Holly-penned 'Not Fade Away', that the Stones had perforated with a wailing disruptive harmonica, squeezing the accelerated beat into mania. Mick Jagger and his piratical guitarist, Keith Richards, had adopted Chuck Berry's trademark duck walk and revamped it as awkward Dartford butch. Jagger's harmonica and Richards' guitar were bending and swooping together, in raw surges of R&B.

The blond one, Brian Jones, was naturally scary, and projected an aloof conceit. Brian had a permanently derisive sneer, and was wired with impacted aggression, like he was inciting every male in the room to hit him. He appeared detached from the band, as though he was contemptuous of their electrifying voodoo, and played virtuoso slide with an arrogance that seemed to resent any sharing of his contribution with the rhythm section.

But no matter the attraction his fixating, paranoid look achieved, the audience's attention always went back to Jagger, not only because he was the front man, but for his compulsively exaggerated dance, and the way he turned his back and wiggled his arse, up on the tips of his toes, like a gay boy, in a way you wouldn't dare imitate, because it was a figure cooked by the skewed Bo Diddley meets Eel Pie beat, that exploded in your face like a garage rehearsal from a middle-class kid from Dartford who was adept at impersonating cockney, and a deep southern drawl, and whose raffish persona was quite obviously a projection of the sweaty music, rather than a rebellious lifestyle.

Jagger was generating unprecedented crowd hysteria on the club circuit, his negroid lips and limp-wristed hand gestures winning girls and boys in equal numbers, as the band stomped provocatively into a rework of 'King Bee', the singer so assured in the authoritative space he opened up round each syllable of his phrasing, that the girls in the front row were infected by a contagious hysteria, an unstoppable sexual impulse to scream deliriously.

## CRAWDADDY 1963

They cut it hot: its one-shoulder-striptease,
the singer's sweater angled girlishly
each time he slows the tempo to a drawl

and sees his image on the mirrored wall
as someone else grown dangerous with power,
a stalker talking blues with maracas,

a dervish improvising a stage prowl.
It's Brian's blues harp shimmers between riffs
creating colours with impromptu speed,

as though each blue demands a variant,
a grey or mauve as textured subtlety.
The drummer's three-piece suit citifies rock

and contrasts with Keith's wolfishly unkempt
appropriation of a waistcoat, jeans,
his Bo Diddley chords so naively tight

they parrot source, but come out garagey.
The crowd's on burn, new blood alive
to a youth gestalt: they are on their knees

instinctively caught up by the tempo,
conflicting factions finding unity
in gestural dance, raw-sexed abandonment

to poppy R&B – the leather boys
dancing with Mods, all warring archetypes
dissolved in a collective energy

at Station Road, the Thames windowing ice,
the singer reinventing masculinity
with pouty, sexless contempt, winning all

by blowing losers clean out of the door,
the rhythm fast, untiring, and the charge
creating the '60s on a dance floor.

## EDITH GROVE

The fungi on the walls are like blue bread,
fist-sized excrescences, crop-circle whorls,
paisley blotches abseiling to the bed.

Mick's gone off with a satchel bricked with books,
the two guitarists strum with cold fingers
to old guttural Muddy Waters hooks.

They poncho blankets. A red winter sun
squeezes an orange over Chelsea docks.
Brian does slide, a riffy trick he's won.

Andrew's in town at Strickland's Record Store,
corner of Dean and Compton, riffling sounds;
the future thumps him like the subway roar.

Soho's all putzah. Johnny Danger's floor's
the third one up. A pink shirt says it all.
It signals access to fire-proofed doors.

Back in the Chelsea den, they cut it raw.
Keith's understudy Buddy Holly licks
break through the jamming like a sudden thaw.

The dishes tower like a Westway high-rise,
a scissored NME rafts on the floor,
small ads circled. Mick's make-up's a surprise –

Max Factor eye-shadows, a blue, a green
left open on the basin, Quant powder
skid-marking the rim with a dusty sheen ...

Nobody loves you when you're down and out.'
The heating's disconnected, room's a tip,
the mess providing the rebellious clout

to foster image – spotty bad boy loons,
defiant, dead broke, stealing guitar picks
and quickly mastering Bo Diddley tunes.

## ANDREW LOOG OLDHAM

Skinny, entrepreneurial zeitgeist,
ex-Epstein, ex-Quant
window dresser, aka Sandy Beach
and Chancery Lane,
names like the feather boa swish
of drag artistes at the Vauxhall Tavern:
blown away at the Crawdaddy
by Jagger's explosive bi-itch,
the Stones' lean-mean attitude
in wiring rock to R&B,
burnt on the moment by their flash
and fielding it as manager,
twitchy in pink hexagonal lenses
and studied eyeliner,
match-mate to Mick's lashed mascara,
rounding up the band's energies
to corral them at Decca,
work on their bad boy lowlife sneer
through Jagger's affected cockney,
hustle for crowd hysteria
to detonate each smashed up show,
moved into Mapesbury Road with Mick
and Chrissie Shrimpton, shared his bed
and make-up and camp repartee,
wrote liner notes surreal as bleach
turned a-syntactical purple,
sold out to Allen Klein, the deal
haemorrhaging profit,
got fried, then wiped by ECT,
a green-lighter disorbiting
in conflagratory mania,
booted into redundancy

like strawberry-haired Brian Jones,
a hard fall, over, under,
sideways, down and out corridor,
a decade-shaper exiting
like a burnt-out meteor.

## REGENT SOUND

A boxy hotel room-sized studio,
stripped ivory paint, the burnt omelette blotches
rashing the walls; a demo-space
in Denmark Street, mono only
for primitives – the Stones in there
bleeding their amps to wall of noise.

The red-haired, tie-thin Dadaist
Impresario – ALO –
works the control room like a test pilot,
the accidental and the found
mixed at a level that's so raw
it detonates ear-drums.

The sounds live and direct-to-disc,
a cobbled blues-punk, teeny rip,
a sonic speedball like a Tyson fist
mashing the gobsmacked Decca head,
a spotty, in your nose, dude-bravura
breaking taboos like digging up the dead.

Jagger's a fire-eating mike-swallower
surfing his breath into the song,
needling it with subjective fangs.
They leak delay into an in-house theme,
a customised state-of-the-art motif.
Small money. Big time. An art student's dream.

Egg boxes for sound baffling, they plug in,
extemporise round an acoustic riff,
then kick a blues storm through 'Not Fade Away'.
The B-side's nailed in twenty minutes flat –
'Little by Little' with its twelve-bar blues
and churlish vocals from a lip curled cat.

They can the songs on credit, pool cab fares,
leave scuff marks from their blue Anello boots,
their moment coming, like they've grown with it
as destiny, a welling up of roots
to meet the age – they take it in their stride –
and notch up a decade of blazing hits.

## CHESS STUDIOS 1964

Muddy Waters paints the ceiling
menthol-green, odd-jobbing slashes
like a naïve emulsioned
Barnett Newman,
shafts a brush in the can.

Charlie's sniffing through the archives
for legendary Chess
45s.
Bill requisitions memorabilia.
Brian slyly sips Wild Turkey.

Five British ingénues
whoop it up in Ron Malo's room,
unnerved by the sound's sharp creases
moptop cowed blues parvenus
cracking through 'Under the Boardwalk',

summery as ripening lemons,
Keith cranks proto-power chords
and loping tangential figures
on Chicago misogyny
a captious 'It's All Over Now',

canned to commandeer the hotspot
as a global No 1.
Muddy drops in, blotched by green blobs
splashed on his dark glasses,
listens gobsmacked to bottleneck

on 'I Can't Be Satisfied'
magicked by the Cheltenham
maestro,
blonde fringe patterned like macramé.
Mick's the part in hounds tooth hipsters,

melismatic tone role-searching
for a viable persona
Cockney slut, intransigent
gigolo, or whisky-shot
Arkansas sharecropper.

# THE STONES AT THE SCENE (2)

The crowd were already shouting for the Stones, with a blood-hot chant of 'Mick' coming like a mantra from the front rows of fangirls leaking infectious hysteria. The club erupted as the band loped on stage, followed by Mick Jagger, his hands on his head, who, on reaching the mic, picked up his yellow maracas, and launched into a tearaway 'I Can't Be Satisfied', the beat caught perfectly as a catch in the seams. It was a cover that sounded even raunchier live, Mick's white tab-collar shirt and skinny silver crew-neck giving him his usual ambiguous girlie take on masculinity as he projected like accelerated vaudeville.

With the two guitarists strutting their stuff, the Stones burnt into 'High-Heeled Sneakers', a number that brought the bottle-blond Brian Jones confrontationally to the edge of the stage, eyes launched to the ceiling distantly, then redirected equally indifferently at the walls, as though, as their founding member, he resented the attention given to other members of the band. He was by turns obnoxious and captivating, but the crowd only had eyes for Mick.

The band took the sound down a level, with the listener-friendly 'Honest I Do', that momentarily softened their outright desperado appeal. Jagger's youthful vulnerability coloured the song, giving him, for the space of three minutes, the deceptive air that he could be the boy next door when he wasn't projecting Mick Jagger. When the crowd surged again, incited by Jagger's pelvic contortions on 'I Just Wanna Make Love to You', Keith Richards targeted an aggressive fanboy's face with the full-on toe-piece of his Anello & Davide Chelsea boot, which crunched his nose-bridge in an arc of blood. It was a hard whack, and those at the front could see that Richards was probably drunk, from the edgy angles at which he was playing. It was clear that things were going to deteriorate rapidly, and the gig was temporarily stopped, before the band came back on and tellingly lit into 'You Can Make It If You Try', as an attempt to cool the atmosphere down, with winning hand gestures, and an easy slow-paced tempo.

With total disdain, the band hit back in with the insurgent 'It's All Right', a fast, flippant statement of self-assertive esteem that the Stones continued in the process of their expansive notoriety. The song worked the room to explosion, as though the band had demonstrably outstripped small club audiences, and needed to move on by the sheer force of their momentum.

The heat and volume were turned right up as the band swooped into their current No 1, 'It's All Over Now', as a marker to close a chaotic gig, the guitars ringing and Mick doing a girlie dance copy of a Vauxhall Tavern travesty as he caught the rhythm of money and fame in his angular projection, the hook delivering misogynistic air-punches at dismissing women, putting them down and in the past, 'And I used to love her/but it's all over now . . .' And the short gig was exhaustively over. The band turned and ran backstage, their gofers forming an intimidating wall to prevent the crowd's concerted efforts to break through.

## AMERICAN TOUR 1964

The highway's longer than Proust's novel,
Route 66 telescopes
like Napoleon
into Russia.
It's like crossing the sky's curve

and stopping off between planets.
A red Chevy eats the road
stereo blasting
Otis Redding.
Brian's six calla lily stems

are heavier than golf clubs
on his black elephant cord lap.
He's a strawberry blonde bobbed
like Audrey Hepburn
carriers stacked up with Stax

and Motown vinyl.
Their tour zeroes as it fans out,
boxy sound cubed in undersold
heat-prickly arenas.
Mick does fame dancing to himself

with mincy steps, as though his feet
are bandaged to retarded stubs
like a Chinese fetish.
His act's from the Vauxhall Tavern
travestying Diana Ross . . .

Backstage, the cops snout .44s
at Keith's up all night eyeballs,
flick his fringe with a baton.
They're roughed up on a gutsy haul,
Detroit, Pittsburgh, Cleveland, LA,

fetching up at Carnegie Hall,
brokering a mini-riot,
sweet success in the Big Apple,
a first bite, the juice so sharp
it burns like whisky from the bottle.

## KICKING IN 1964

90. The English summer spoils to drought.
London turns mirage, Hampshire's grizzled blonde
slashed by red poppies: everywhere the land

shoulders its raw defensives—dust and stone.
They're slammed across motorway gradients,
cooking assault on small towns, targeting

resistance with hormonal-soup,
slapping maracas to a muddy beat,
the voodoo-tempo working like a hex...

The hall at Plymouth's on impacted heat,
explosive tension layer by layer stripped down
to optimal hysterics, dementia

that surfs the crowd in pheromonal waves
peaking in a front row that surfs the stage,
chair legs ripped off as splintered weaponry...

The band do motions with their instruments,
their sound inaudible, their gestural quirks
suggesting counter-terrorists

doing Kabuki behind police helmets,
protected from the riot they incite,
by a bottled, beat-up constabulary:

each number ripped into dismemberment.
It's life and death, and they're prepared to run
at the first break in the blue barrier,

the first knife-in-the-teeth vengeful weirdo
whose girl loves Brian, and whose vaulting leap
projects him headfirst at the microphone.

## BURN

Keith's slept-in hair's their signature
a profile like Cro-Magnon crow
picking chords on a ruined hotel bed.

They're roomed up at the City Motor Lodge,
the all-American clouds breeze over
like Wall Street data on a thermal high.

Bottled by an antagonist
Brian's skull lesion's like the Grand Canyon
boiling with paranoia.

Keith's been electrocuted, chainsaw buzzed
at Sacramento, bolted flat,
laid out on stage, his hush puppies

doing their insulating trick.
Mick wears white Capezio ballet shoes
to androgenise sophomores.

Charlie's like a bespoke Taoist,
a savant whose brushes dictate
circadian rhythm to the beat.

Bill's bass licks play descending stairs,
the way down always the way up.
He builds a wall into their melody.

They've shed R&B and soul skins
for folk rock armour, upped their clout
as meanies with an attitude.

They craft their future in four days
compressed studio time, tool their best
and instantaneous Aftermath

at RCA, flaked out behind locked doors
with Brian dubbing harpsichord
that gentle it's like manicure.

## MARIANNE FAITHFULL (1)

The King's Road gamine iconised
by rock bon vivants, zipping it
in a shimmied Mustang Sally.

Chelsea's a cornucopia
of frothy boutiques: she'll load up
at Granny Takes a Trip

or riffle Biba's simmery
fantasia for plum velvets,
a crochet mini-skirt.

A demi-monde chanteuse, her songs
are fragile, flock-wallpaper things,
no hint yet of their tortured grab.

Spliffy bohemianism rules
the quality; at Courtfield Road
Brian Jones is a petit-four

placed on a cerise cushion.
The elect drive Rolls', invest
in serendipitous antiques.

She's Jagger's blousy rock chick
feted, thrown into the air
like customised confetti.

The drugs are Smarties with a kick,
they make her see her own TV
as substance commentary.

The party lasts for a decade,
the guests get reinvented, die,
or stare at the King's Road transformed

by update, like a corridor,
revamped, redecorated, framed
for a new cortège to pass through.

## THE LAST TIME

The LA sunshine's coded 1965,
arrived at 736,000 miles per second
to polish a hotel window
with a pink and green rainbow
tracking a rhomboid on a late sleeper

surfacing in a mashed and clothes-spilled bed,
guitar cases stashed on the floor,
the blonde beside him sitting up
checking the autograph on her left arm
and in a peach-flush shimmying for the shower...

Later, the band convene at RCA,
a cleaner sweeps the studio's parquet floor,
they have all three, A, B and C,
high white ceilings and live echo chambers,
gobos for spectators, metal doors,

Neumann and Telefunken microphones,
a Neve console, ALO's hunch
building the audio layers with guitars
on a loping, hypnotic 'The Last Time',
punchy with its contagious hook...

Phil Spector livewires in to hear the sound,
maroon suit, mirrored Chelsea boots,
he wants to face it volume up,
tunnel clean through the sonic corridor
and pitch himself at its monitored core...

He stays behind, plays bass on 'Play With Fire',
the morning sun blasting tomato red
over a 4am Sunset Boulevard,
the studio cleaner got into the mix,
brushing in corners, echo on each sweep.

# THE STONES AT THE SCENE (3)

The Stones were coming on so raw that Keith Richards' fingers were bleeding from the velocity at which he hit the chords. The impulsive, unrehearsed music was stunning for its reliance on an amalgam of Blues, R&B, Soul and Rock and Roll, all slammed together by an invasive poppiness that was dirty, Thames-muddy and right in your face. The band slouched into the down-mooded 'Pain in My Heart', monopolised by Jagger's insolent tone, the harmonica he blew squeezed like a distraught Juicer pulping an orange to Blues. The texture of the playing, the elegiac surges coming from some place in Jagger's head that wasn't Dartford but an osmotic Chess Studios Chicago Blues.

High-octane energy bands like The Who, The Animals, and The Action had performed at the Scene but there was nothing comparable to the Stones, and the slash of anarchic energy they generated was ripping up the boards with each number. The guitarists had developed a way of deliberately taking their time tuning between songs, the calculated delay, inciting hostility from the front. Richards had turned the volume up to max, as the Stones launched into a raunchy 'Down in the Bottom', gunning the audience with sonic assault, the singer's naturally exuberant bounce maintaining perfect pitch on a Muddy Waters' number needing adroit piloting to keep the snappy time.

The bassist played supernumerary notes, a diminutive, absolutely immobile figure, chewing gum and staring up at the ceiling, as though he really wasn't part of the unit, and was way too old for the teenage affront projected by Jagger's unstoppable lip. Bill Wyman wasn't plugged into the same energies, he seemed redundant to pop, more like a plumber who had a sideline interest in the Blues, while the drummer was the paradigm of Ivy League, his ivory mohair suit pulled from Austin's on Shaftesbury Avenue, his white tab-collar shirt and candy-striped loyal-blue and lipstick-red tie, emphasising his cool panache, and his timing perfect, harnessing the whole rhythmic infrastructure to a tight precisional beat. He was the one in the band who sartorially was undeniably Mod. There was something oriental about his imperturbable, deadpan features, his heavily lidded eyes, and his unswerving professionalism to what he was doing on his kit in a sweaty Soho cellar.

There was a technical hitch that left the Stones in disconnect for a few minutes, anxious not to lose momentum, and looking tired under the lights, as though the exhaustion of playing two sets a night on provincial tours was starting to be mapped into their features. Brian Jones, particularly, looked collapsed inside, his face submerged by a series of epidermal foot-wells, descending from dark-blue eye pouches, into obviously debauched features. When the power came back on, the band initiated a breezy 'Little by Little', still another song in their repertoire that was outright misogynistic, and seemed part of their collective attitude of disdain for women in general.

The room temperature was malarial, swampy, in a cellar overtaken by a scorching, upbeat tribal frenzy. In the heat of it all, Jagger's art appeared one of unusual detachment, as though he wasn't in any way culpable for the storm he had created. It was this volatile, appetently sexual, impersonator's oomph, in contrast to an essentially aloof aesthetic, that had the crowd hooked. The band by now seemed slightly intimidated naturals to the adulatory response given them that kept on building, like shock-waves, through the black-walled basement, in a West End that was accelerating into the Mod capital. The noise they created seemed to envelop them in a defensive, fuzzy halo of sound.

Without warning, the band fired into the Chuck Berry rocker 'Around and Around', a Rock tornado that got the singer and the whole floor boiling with whipped-up energies that had the floor and ceiling spin in opposite directions, the impact was so immediate. If the playing was basic, then the cover was stitched together by

Mick Jagger's idiosyncratic hustler's tone, as though he was endorsing the black underclass through a privileged white empathy, while cleverly representing neither.

Jagger unexpectedly and provocatively slowed the tempo right down by announcing, and loping into, the moody, slouched beat of 'You Better Move On', a hypnotic, slow-burn Willie Alexander number. They closed with their recent chart-topping Bobby Womack cover 'It's All Over Now', a declarative, chord-ringing 12-string winner, that sounded so urgently modern that the audience could feel the speed of the times in the choppy riff, that was still pop, no matter its Blues sources. The song really brought the band together as an act without rivals, the hook creating a Scotch-and-soda mix with the teeny audience, who danced crazily to make a dissolve into the sound. It seemed like even the cellar walls were moving to the accelerated beat, and that Mick Jagger had arrived as the seminal voice to whatever generational rebelliousness circulated in hot youthful blood in 1964. The Stones ran on the last lick, the wedged heels of their Chelsea boots reverberating across the boards in their frantic dash, not for the dressing room, where on earlier dates they had signed autographs for fans, but for the rear exit, where a mirror-stripped, lipstick-van was waiting to get them out of the yard, like criminals on the run.

## BRIAN'S OFF THE WALL

Another desultory three-star hotel,
Britain reviewed from limos, Bradford seen
from the hard shoulder of the motorway...

Their haul's provincial. Brian's airline bag
contains the evidence, his whiskey pact
feeding a malt to his dependent's need –

a bottle a day gone AWOL
replenished with chunky Scottish-clan brands,
the empties body-bagged like casualties...

It's pressure in his nerves blows fuses out,
his epileptic blackouts, seizures, fits,
his panic arriving with the choked roar

of a tube's build-up and braked counter thrust.
Each day the same reckless fan-crazed assault,
ripped jacket, violated shirt and hair,

marauding offensives, a twisted fist
aimed for the jaw, a rocky getaway,
the car jostled by an opposing wall

of mini-skirted hysterics, teenies
mad on the image and 'Not Fade Away'.
Brian's the capricious all-hours drinker,

the bibulous sophisticat left out
of band meetings, the solitary deposed
leader turned nervy, disinherited

of a rock-kingdom, as they slide through wet
towards another cut-short date, the night
building behind them as blue swaggy cloud.

## PLAY WITH FIRE

Take a blues man and he colours
choked gospel deep South
as though a carp turned over

in refracted depths
flush in a pond
cool fire bleeding orange . . .

Elmore James, Chuck Berry,
Bo Diddley, Willie Dixon,
plaintively grainy numbers

slouch-voiced, drawlish raw,
each lament protested
from a subterranean cellar.

Blues cracks the voice
like lived-in leather
roughed out Muddy Waters

and insolent Jagger
sparking up Negroid
on Little Red Rooster

hanging out the notes
like offensives on a line
then licking them with breath

and punchy harmonica
arrogant the white boy way
of giving blues a sex change.

## AFTERMATH

1

On Mother's Little Helper, Jagger's sneer
denouncing age is counterpoint
to fine wrinkles drawn from a sitar.

2

Stupid Girl's uncurtailed misogyny,
the singer means it with his venomous
jabby vocal authority.

3

Brian's twinkly dulcimer on Lady Jane
works through the song texture like a red carp
nudging a still pond after rain.

4

Marimbas as the subtext to she's dumb,
the lippy thermal the real dominant
in pressing home Under My Thumb.

5

The slide guitar's so dreamy it's film-scored
into a tetchy Doncha Bother Me,
the singer acting petulantly bored.

6

A bluesy, wailing, foghorned signature,
the harmonica's phrase on Goin' Home
sounds like it's squeezed out of the underworld.

7

Flight 505 punches imperatives
out of a crisp ensemble – departure gates
jumpy like bees around a hive.

8
A tight-lipped reappraisal, High and Dry
plays out a breezy emotional tide-mark;
a rock pool bottled with blue sky.

9
She's lost her moment, like a stiletto,
the obsolete girl on Out of Time
chipped off like red gloss on a toe.

10
The sweet and sharp of youthful loneliness
wrung into It's Not Easy permeate
the song like scent on a flimsy dress.

11
The perfect stranger sits in every bar,
a plaintive I Am Waiting mirrors change
like a face sighted from a speeding car.

12
Jagger's the polished apple and the core,
Take It Or Leave It has dismissive threat
to someone crawling back for more.

13
Think's a résumé, the sub-aqueous sax
recalling hard times bettered, moving on,
but keeping blues roots in the mix.

14
Equivocations: What To Do spells gain
to the protagonist: he'll think her back
for reappraisal in the London rain.

## SUN GOING DOWN (ON ME)

Mid-decade's the high water mark –
the Stones in 1965
washed by angry undertow,
a tentacular feeler
twitching an adhesive lasso

round Brian's jugular,
dragging on a manager
whose liner notes are proto-punk
*Clockwork Orange* cocktailed
with up yours yahoo.

They've scrapped 'Could You Walk On Water?'
for its messianic archetype.
Lennon crossed the Mersey
the salt on his toes
a filigree stigmata?

Jagger drops in at the Chelsea
in a black and white check suit.
Dylan's too stoned to look up,
contemplating a fragment
written on his boot.

The day comes up everywhere,
only the sun's oranger,
the summer bluer at Southend,
Brighton and Honolulu.
The dead are counted in the air.

Oldham's clinging to a cork
skating in the deep end,
his bipolar disorder
disrupts his chemistry and peaks
like a mid-air disaster . . .

Brian's dodgy, hatching plots,
legless, slurry, out of it.
The sixties shift like changing chords,
a figure held and lost again
like sunshine after early-morning rain.

## COURTFIELD ROAD

The sausage trampolines in fat,
fork-pronged cholesterol spatter
an ingenuous groupie twists
in sizzling batter –
a mid-morning brunchy affair,
the kitchen a graveyard of caked dishes
randomly highrised, gunked and slewed
to deviated minarets.
He's upstairs in the gallery
affecting a gold kimono,
cross-legged, his blue eyes cancelled out
by mental trouble, free-floater
hallucinatory tableaux.
Le petit mal dusts his aura
with disconnection, black-outs, faze.
He's deconstruction to himself,
his hand plotting a whisky glass
like complex chess played
with the bottle. Two tulle sunflowers
impose quasi-ecology
on the lowlight interior.
Brian tinkles a tambourine
to compensate for emptiness
with little twinkling flurries.
He feels like a light-exposed negative,
the image dematerialised
inside an ectoplasmic frame.
His crackly vinyls are de-sleeved,
clothes litter every chair, bright silks
and velvets ruined at the seams.
The groupie punishes his snakeskin boots,
bats at the fry-up's hissy squish
of popping frazzles, bacon, eggs,

a sunset-squally tomato,
pops buttons on a satin shirt
filched from a drawer, and contemplates
the maestro's used-up, flash-fired youth,
his untogether zero-impetus
keeping him moody, as she tips
anchor-shaped mushrooms on two raunchy plates.

## THE STONES AT THE SCENE (4)

The crowd was pushing out the black-painted walls in anticipation, as the band came on to a perfected, seamlessly tight 'Have Mercy' played with proficient, exhilarating cool; Mick Jagger's voice and handclaps arrogating over a sound pulled by the blue umbilical from the Deep South into a sweaty Soho cellar. This time Jagger was wearing a tomato-red skinny crew-neck jumper over black-and-white hound's-tooth check hipsters, with a slash of neon-red lipstick.

Brian Jones was dressed all in white; white polo neck, white jeans and white shoes, and his mint green and white Vox Phantom Teardrop guitar seemed like an extension of his neurology in the way that he held it, as an intelligent part that resonated from fine-tuned pathways in his brain. He looked incurably ill, as though chronic stress, or too many exhaustively late nights, had got cocktailed into his tired blood, and disinterested, as though he really didn't connect with the others as a virtuoso colourist, and stood right up, apart, dissociated, on the lip of the stage.

Richards was his usual piratical self, playing three-chord guitar with a ring so basic it was fundamental Blues worked into Rock and pop riffs, without really being any of them, other than his own self-taught, workmanlike genre of playing. He was outwardly the most relaxed on stage, and the most dangerous: he was the taciturn band member who kicked people's teeth out, and broke guitars over unsuspecting promoters' heads.

It was common knowledge that the bass player, inanely chewing gum, was provincially married, and that the drummer was to follow, facts that left many totally disinterested in their apparently conventional lives. They seemed blank supernumeraries by way of contrast to the manically edgy guitarists, meshing into each other's musical diaphragms, and the singer's bamboo-skinny outré projection, soaked in a sexual ambiguity that wrecked all preconceived notions of gender.

The Stones literally smooched into their fourth and highest placed US single, 'Time Is On My Side', an Irma Thomas B-side, recorded at Chess, that slowed the temperature to a moody, reflective one, in which the band appealingly iced the original, like a drizzled lemon cake, topped with orange and vanilla. The upbeat rhythm was quickly restored for a catchy, throwaway, self-penned number, announced as 'Off the Hook', a song that provided Jagger with the welcome opportunity to throw inimitably camp gestures.

When the band temporarily stopped playing to tune, the interlude of quiet was like orgasm, only a matter of acute seconds, before the band exploded into 'I'm All Right', an unruly fracas of shaken maracas and loopy guitar energies, driven home with a vocal authority that nailed the rhythm to the beat. The band were clearly so rehearsed, from playing two gigs a night, that their timing was precisionally tight, and so hot, that they sounded like guitar sex, with a drawlish vocal guide. They pulled you right into the music like an aural event horizon, and they were, notoriously, starting to get rich from it, in a way that most Mod bands weren't, like they had overtaken the club circuit, and left everybody a thousand miles down the road as oily garage hands.

When they lit into a tribally urgent 'Not Fade Away', made mean and urgent at Buddy Holly's expense, they gunned the audience into a collective storm whipped up by the song's minimally compacted immediacy.

The band picked up again with their favourite, 'Carol', a Chuck Berry scorcher, converted into their own idiosyncratic garage flavour, with the song consolidating their gangish suzerainty of the London circuit with DIY Fender amps, a sound system so inadequate it boxed them into primitive tribalism, and as five desperados, so full-on in their looks and sound, it sounded like they were playing directly in a living room.

Sensing from the turbulent crowd response that they had outlived their stay, Jagger angled into a killer 'King Bee', all hips and lippy pouts, his hands wrapped round his waist, like a woman liming measured, his unrepentant manner taking the form of a finger admonishing the audience. The number was a slouch, played almost like crypto-burlesque, with Jagger's dance-steps pivoting on toe-points, and the girls starting to break rows and push for the stage. There was a concerted rush forward, as though the whole club projected its insane, sexed-up dynamic at the band, like a thrust of Boeing turbos, and the Stones were running helter-skelter for their lives backstage in a flurry of abrasive boot heels.

## PAINT IT BLACK

Cooking like thunder
behind soufflé cumulus
the shock's the sitar's
elegiac attack,
a jangly Berber dissonance

of movable frets
colouring a signature
that's dejectedly black,
the motif so hooky
it jumps out like a pivotal

switch in direction
to a try-out decade,
the Stones turned funereal,
introspectively eclipsed,
seeing colour through brain fade

as ubiquitous black.
A chart-fêted ensemble
turned perverse with themselves,
nihilistic, reversionary,
squeezed the moment like an orange

of its Vit C elixir,
swung round on the King's Road
and saw the sun black.
Wind blew out of the summer
sparky with planetary glitter

inciting guitars
to register change.
Brian's jingly fingers
damaged in Tangier
no longer instructive

to baroque inflections,
closed down with Aftermath,
his tinkling recherché
prettified embellishments
sacrificed for raunchier hits.

## MOROCCAN INTERLUDE

A coyote wail
of power-chords over the casbah
howls from the Minzah's
immaculate tenth floor,
promises of Jajouka

entailed over kif
or majoun in a hookah,
Brion Gysin's caduceus
pointing up to the mountains
where Targuisti and Salah

confab with the tribe.
Brian's going ballistic
beating Anita
and bringing back Berbers
with tattoos on their vulvas...

Paul Bowles given entrée
noodles in for tea,
taciturn, saturnine,
in an ivory linen suit
he beats a fast retreat...

Cecil Beaton's fixated
by Mick's derrière
and how he angles a finger
smoking like Dietrich,
orchestrating a Stuyvesant

like a trout fisher
lobbying a fly.
Mick dances for his mincey
spectatorial sugar daddy's
royal demeanour,

a queeny voyeur
perfect as a calla
lily in a Ming vase,
wearing a Harrods green silk tie
in the desert heat.

Keith drives off with Anita
in his chauffeured Blue Lina,
the party gone cool,
like a jinn dumped pollutants
in the green swimming pool.

Brian's pilled up, hysterical,
left behind.
Beaton sniffs at a red rose
held like a powder puff
to his fine-boned nose.

## HOTEL MINZAH

A coven at the Minzah
jajouka's understudy
delusionally schizoid –
twitchy Brian Jones
vamped in Berber jewellery
high on Elmore James
and all broken down

The whole Stones party
room-in to the music's
gutsy bluesy wail
Brian's asthma-panicked
weirded from occult
speak of death by water
and all broken down

Tangier smells of hashish
Paul Bowles as expat guru
lighting up a hookah
Brian's neurotoxic
sees his hands as flippers
sheeny as frog skin
and all broken down

All those Ossie Clark
gold brocaded coats
rupture at the seams
Mick's gone to the mountains
Brian's on the flat
plateaued in brooding
and all broken down

Paranormal quirks
keep on quizzing Brian
he's scared goose-pimplish
his killer's on his back
disguised as black on black
a hit man in an alley
and all broken down.

## KEITH RICHARDS 1967

He's doped into unfazed passivity –
a blackout, roomed-up, quirky indolence,

a cool alert to inspirational riffs
that flicker through his foggy chemistry;

the way that 'Satisfaction' jumped from sleep
into a declamatory guitar phrase,

a buzzily infectious instant hook...
He's cooked by ennui, blanket lethargy,

this raffish squire in buskins moonishly
baffled by sunlight leaking through a blind.

He's prototypical 'go get a life
if you're not me,' his scissor-legs stage style

an exercise in smart audacity –
a poppishly upgraded B.B. King.

He's schooled by ear, those days at Edith Grove
listening to vinyl wear in canyoned grooves

tracking to gutturally raw Elmore James.
He airguns water rats by a souped moat,

his deerhound Syphilis shampooed by spray...
His liquor intake's like a disappearing trick,

the measure of an invisible sea
that drops and rises trafficking empties.

He's the survival-paradigm,
not closed, but looking out, holding the flow

of hot riffs in his livered blood,
pumping instinctual beat into a sound

building its own long-arc trajectory
over the waiting in five continents.

## THE ROLLING STONES' AESTHETIC

Aesthetically, the Stones represented a mixture of outright ugly and androgynous appeal. The bassist was a dead loss, the drummer too, in terms of visual appeal; they had back-wall faces, without any redeeming look, while the frontline, and most of all Mick, had a rude ambivalent quality, above all modern, in a way that integrated street-cred into the possible diagnostics of good looks. They were essentially rebels, had been groomed to cultivate punk as cool and had taken to it naturally, while making it clear that they were still acceptable to their families.

The Stones did uncoordinated fashion: they downgraded style into draggy separates – bits of Carnaby Street worn with Ivy League from Justin's, and pastel cashmere jumpers that belonged to girlfriends and ubiquitous high heel Chelsea boots with Cuban heels from Anello and Davide. Their shirts were picked selectively from John Stephen, Cecil Gee and John Michael.

In a month, the media had hyped the Stones' adopted bad boy image into a sensationalised furore. The *Melody Maker* headline: 'Would you let your daughter marry a Rolling Stone?' was a caption controversially engineered, on his own admission, by their dodgy, entrepreneurial manager, Andrew Loog Oldham, as unprecedented PR.

The Stones, in their white tab-collared dress shirts, and Cecil Gee Italian-styled jackets, the backbeat always coming in a fraction late, the meshed guitars tight but sloppy, were most notably an untutored joining of strengths that came together as a chaotic mix.

The Stones did a mean studio set at Camden Theatre, as part of the series *Blues in Rhythm*, hosted by Long John Baldry, where they played with all of their primitive blues energies on contagiously hooky numbers like 'Mona', 'Cops and Robbers', and the hypnotic slow tempo 'You Better Move On', that fitted Jagger's voice like a blue glove. The show was a taster of the band's accelerated professionalism, the tightness of their playing, the way the lead and rhythm guitars meshed now like tying shoelaces, and then there was Jagger's sluttish strut, his queeny steps crossing each other as an exaggerated mince, his hands fitting his hips like a burlesque stripper.

## KEITH RICHARDS' RHYTHM TRICK

A slide pickup in 1962,
a cheap f-hole guitar for trafficking
Chicago blues, Bo
Diddley, Chuck Berry, just paying dues
to growling blues myths, journeying

through Howlin' Wolf and B.B. King,
meshing with Brian's edgy chords,
lead and rhythm doing counterpoint.
Later the licks are open tunings:
D, A, D, F, A, D low

to high, like Twenties, Thirties blues,
nothing on paper, played by ear,
a high string tuned an octave lower.
Style's his paterfamilias
grown in him like rings on a tree,

seasoned, understudied grain.
Tooling a Gibson J-200,
Nashville strung, a ringy 12-string,
he lays down at Muscle Shoals
Alabama, a feel-good, crisp

as crackly bacon 'Brown Sugar'.
Custom made by Newman Jones
his five-string guitar organises
huckster figures, aluminium neck
cushioned by red varnished maple.

Fingerprints with claw-hammer,
works a scorched little finger
playing bottleneck with glass
from a green Heineken bottle,
gets the sound with inimitable class.

Uses a small studio amp
to think big, and plots by ear
a pattern that gives infrastructure
to a phrase, and builds on it
his bluesy individual signature.

## NERONIAN

Heliogabalus, Caligula, Nero,
despotic, transvestite psychos
fisting out jewels like Campana hailstones,

emeralds cool as deep water;
draggily made-up in ostrich feathers,
self-divinised, flexing a leashed leopard

en route to a same-sex sauna.
Heliogabalus peppers the 60s
with orgiastic aphrodisia

a Jagger/Richards/Jones androgyny,
bibbed satin shirts, UFO-like ascot hats,
a drug-fest saturnalia,

the limos stagy as hearses,
a rear-seat groupie ostentatiously
pouting with a red lipstick gash,

somebody spooning caviar
from its post-cryogenic state
into a slippery tasting palate.

Reckless excess in Chelsea,
Byronic lotharios in velvet
turn night into day with amyl nitrate,

eulogise the unending party.
Decadent patricians reincarnate
in the exalted glitterati,

the boy-gods stadiumed again
with feedback and a microphone,
like the Stones in a froggish armoured car

nudging to the swollen amphitheatre,
the crowds hysterical, the thrown roses
the sunset-red of the assassin's mark.

## WORMWOOD SCRUBS

Richards banged up – the 19th-century cell
sits on him like a concrete
turtle shell,

a chair, a pencil and paper
to write 'Dear mother,
da-da-da,'

his amygdala
switched to fear, a blunt-edged spoon
reflecting a tinny moon,

the little window set up high
admitting a blue rectangle
of cloudy summer sky

cancelled that afternoon to grey.
A lifer drops him tobacco –
a knuckle like a gold nugget

of Golden Flake; the prisoners rap
camaraderie on his door,
one year written on him like a tattoo,

he does compulsory in the yard,
the prison collects an eruptive roar
of stomping applause worked up floor by floor

for 'Satisfaction'. Mug shot done,
paranoia creeps like a waterline
notching up its ascendancy.

Later, the news: he's out on bail:
jump-starting freedom, kicking at the door,
leaving historic boot marks on the wall.

## BRIXTON PRISON

The fetid squalor has him gag,
the archetypal bad boy
used to a red leather upholstered Jag

monitored by a twitchy screw
Jagger's the tiger in a cage,
stripped of his belt, bracelet and rings,

brushed by the warder's eye, as though
the man would beam him dead.
His pencil's the trajectory

to planets rayed across the galaxy.
He feeds the paper scrambled lines
of dithyrambic poetry,

flinches at his grey uniform,
scents danger in his cell-mate's
uncoordinated glower.

He's there for non-prescription speed –
four blue synergised offenders,
methyl amphetamine hydrochloride –

mother's little helpers.
He's wreckage, like a plane shot down
in free fall over London.

He's cut back, a cause célèbre,
fielded by Tom Driberg's pro-gay
defiance of the Commons . . .

Summer's outside like a silk dress
rewarding curves.
It's orangey 1967.

They work to get him out on bail.
Time's jumped ahead and he's behind,
busy again, anxious to sniff the real.

## HANG FIRE (EUROPE 1967)

Brian's slinged arm's like a clubfoot
an orthopaedic jackboot
doing a clumsy thoracic salute.

At Malmo there's a riot
they slow by playing 'Lady Jane'
like singing Thomas Wyatt.

Europe's student zeitgeist
pumps a batoned iron fist
at the bespoke and caviarred

Moet & Chandon commissar.
In Paris they're searched by a functionnaire
smelling like a Pigalle bar's

stock of Provencal Ricard.
In Warsaw, riot police bludgeon
students like they're gutting sturgeon.

Honski de boyski boisk
zee Rollingstonzki.
Brian does his imitation Nazi.

Each border-check's an obligatory strip,
an unsanctioned mind-police
psyching into axons, dendrites.

A smoke bomb Etnas in the hall,
its mushrooming opacity
silencing the jungle roll

of Charlie's tribal bongo.
Their rhythm's the epicentre
of the revolution's core,

hot licked pounding incantations
feeding the molten tsunami
with a bushfire's thunder roar.

# THE ROLLING STONES LIVE

The Stones couldn't sustain a set; the club pulled them off every time in the interests of security after twenty minutes. You had both sexes coming out in the space of a song. It wasn't just the defiantly red lipstick-gashed singer in the silver crew neck jumper and breathed on white hipsters, it was also the partly sneering, bobbed guitarist, hidden by an eye-level blond fringe, who periodically slapped the audience in the face with his tambourine, that ramped up the crowd response to maximum R&B. The Jagger phenomenon, gauche, sexy, impersonating and optimally camp, was devastatingly inimitable, for he represented authentic, mincing, streetwise aggro.

The band were going down a storm at the Flamingo, Eel Pie Island, the Marquee, the Richmond Station Hotel, the Ricky Tick Club, and had successfully charted with their recently released first single, the Chuck Berry cover 'Come On', polarising their characteristic, muddy, accelerated sound to Andrew Loog Oldham's boxy Regent Studio garage production.

Burning into an atonal version of Chuck Berry's 'Carol', the singer characteristically rose on his toes in a piece of pointed drag, to work his angularly pointed hips at the audience, before using the microphone like fellatio.

The Stones were an edgy pub band with a red-haired pioneering manager who wore makeup; but the singer was something else. He had a vamp's insolent projection; he could control the crowd with the bat of an eyelash. He was London's anorexic answer to Elvis without the looks – a pouty renegade Dartford kid, with attitude, who was a natural at pushing edge.

An excited crowd had assembled early in the anticipation of an impromptu Stones gig at the Scene. Those present had kept up with the band's sensational hoopla for notoriety, and in particular the shocking media coverage of their concert at Blackpool's Empress Ballroom on 24 July 1964, at which Keith Richards had activated a riot by kicking a member of the audience in the head with the impacted velocity of his stacked boot heel. There was that, and widely publicised rumours of Brian Jones' scandalous promiscuity; the Brigitte Bardot hairstyled guitarist having in the meantime bought an ostentatious menthol-green and white Vox Phantom Teardrop guitar to add to his role of sensitive colourist to the band's raw garage pyrotechnics.

The Stones were now their own best publicists: they trashed the joint wherever they played, and were recognised as Rock's indomitable bad boys, sitting on top of the charts with their 'Five By Five' EP, recorded at the legendary Chess Studios, Chicago; the mid-tempo Blues of 'If You Need Me', and 'Empty Heart' getting rapidly programmed into the crowd's neural tune-bank, as hooky heart-stoppers. It was summer pop, a distinctly London sound, incongruously dug from the Blues' resources of their delta influences; Muddy Waters, Howlin' Wolf and Chuck Berry, and made so modern it pulled people in like they'd never heard music before.

## BRIAN JONES TRIPS

Psychotic repartee –
the drug answers back
in sci-fi imagery
excerpted from Mars?
as weirdly morphed scrambles

of panicked imagery.
His hand won't unclam
a Ventolin inhaler's
talismanic properties:
he digs in his hold.

The minder can't manoeuvre
Brian to his Rolls:
studio time is real time
he blankwalls, defers
the sleek haul to Barnes.

LSD's the crazies
to his zapped chemistry:
black popping spiders
laboriously track his skin
routing his epidermis

to find a way in.
He's bad-trip invaded
by arachnid avengers
little beady eyes
like headlights on his thorax

turning meteoric,
orange, yellow, red,
explosively eruptive,
the fire in his head
wind-stormed through the flat.

Visual turns audio
with voices in the pipes
natterishly conspiratorial
to his bubbling paranoia
they'll throw him out the window.

His cold sweat bumps hot
from psychoactive toxins,
Brian with a red guitar
and pink velvet suit
gesturally defensive

paralysed with fear
missing out another session
as virtuoso colourist,
already the delinquent,
gone missing, legendary star.

## SATANIC ADVOCATES

Jagger's the morning glory vined
to a decade's toxicity
the chemicals grown saturnine,
spacily mind-altering
acid a visionary gateway

to the garden's underworld,
'Sympathy For the Devil's drapes
on mid-sixties floral pop,
all the dandelion-faced hippies
basementing themselves on smack

gone down a dark corridor
curated by the criminal
sunglassed insiders to the law:
Brian Jones undercover,
harassed, pushed into a fall . . .

The garden's lost its summer daze
its psilocybin rainbow
diffused over every park:
the King's Road darkens along noon,
something's waiting in the sun.

The Stones are blacker limousined
drugs and occult in their blood
Richards a ceremonial
cocktailer of substances,
curtains drawn across the day,

wasted, bean-stringy on speed.
Mostly it goes degenerative
the age's burnt neurology,
all its druggy casualties
sucked to a psychotic core.

The music's hard-edged, rockier,
rumours of disbandment, the blonde
retreating to a Cotchford farm,
death-bound, scenting day by day
his sacrificial murder.

## THEIR SATANIC MAJESTIES REQUEST

She heats a pin and sticks it through a doll
as crude voodoo, intestinal jab
that's gut and liver, imprecates his name –

the blonde one diabolised by her kink.
The band scratches at psychedelic-tech,
a fuzzy electronic vaudeville,

guitar-spook buried in mellotron swirls,
as though the prankster hidden in the song
was Humpty Dumpty sitting on a wall . . .

Court cases nagging in their nerves, they wire
their newly channelled Faustian energies
to off-tilt numbers, svelte Moroccan drums,

the apprehension of bells, rattles, gongs,
textural fade-out and fade-in harmonies.
The flavour's rainbow, churning blues and mauves

banded to citric orange, broody green,
an acid spectrum translating the times
to chemical palette, a jamboree

of wizards hats, faux magic cooked by drugs.
The music points a finger at its source
a rehashed Sgt Pepper lacking stripes,

a ludic playground romp, a finger wag
at the city's Square Mile. Now they invest
defiant image with experiment,

and cocktail tinkling flourishes around
a savage core, play with it and resolve
to kill the soft dynamic that they've found.

## SKEWED

Brian's guitar-dead. His fingers bleed
on picking. A foundation smear
smudges peach on black cashmere
like a residual meteor
got by putting on a face.

He crashes from another space
disorbiting into orbit.
His lisp has a fur collar
like pussy willow.
He's pieces that no longer fit.

He's tea and drugs at four.
A China White Point and strawberries
peppered with hash.
His public school entourage slum
in Chelsea on trust funds and stash.

He's six years old inside his head,
blows harp into a microphone,
but gets no sound,
spends three capitulatory hours
putting a reed into a saxophone.

Vodka's like his swimming pool
a recreational gateway to
seeing things down under.
He tastes Russia in each antiseptic hit
and its moon-sized rye estates.

He's a passenger in a band
harnessed to global long haul.
He's snitched his tie in raspberry yoghurt.
Sometimes he can't separate out
the use of a foot from a hand.

He's fame and pins it on his sleeve.
His birthday cake's shaped like a pink gravestone.
He parties with it, it's pink snow,
goes back to Olympic and finds
he's locked out of the studio.

## CROSSFIRE HURRICANE

They're punked-up,
rebarbative energy-hustlers;
Jagger's market stall bawl – 'it's awwright' –
and it's hot
a lyric that's snarly, stroppily themed

from a Shakespeare plot
a volume turned up
Tempest rehash, a body fished out
on a desert island, beached
and reborn

with recalcitrant lip.
The singer's complaint's invective
in descant,
a post-spike-through-the-head
resurrection, off-centre sung

vituperative whiplash
at a vampirical mother
her witchy antics
zapping his genes,
but still imparting flash

to his hotwire recovery...
The riff's authentic smart,
so driven in
it hurts with neat authority,
so hooky it's on save

as instantaneous catch.
The band in execution
cut it clean
as laser surgery, a phrase
stitched into memory,

a two-chord carnal mantra
pumping like adrenalin.
They're in their moment, on its rush,
and can it 1968
as a compact exigency –

a three-minutes rock novella
chaptered as aural synthesis,
a streamlined waspish guitar bash
laying it down explosively
for vocal kill; 'Jumpin' Jack Flash'.

## BEGGARS BANQUET

A muddy current permeates the blues,
a raw earth country flavoured undertow
chopped by guitars into a racier

discourse with life picked out along a seam
of youth resisting age, rejecting death,
confused, churned up, but finding clarity

in texturing a song with overbite.
Brian's a stress-bleached hoodoo effigy
shot through with hex pins, propped in a booth,

his bottleneck narrating rooty chords
dragged out like water-lilies from a pond,
notes bleeding in a black mood finale.

Mostly nocturnal work. Olympic. Barnes.
The register's a pummelled knucklish swipe
at hierarchy: they cut it fast and slow,

these brash reminders they are like a sea
advancing on the age, deep tidal push
smashing the props from 1968...

'No Expectations' bares a skeleton,
it's Brian's riff picks flesh off his bones,
as though he played by ear posthumously.

Richards lays skewed foundations to each song,
a schema for the singer's overview
in claiming luciferian attributes,

a quippy, giant-arena metaphor
for burning hot, shouldering a decade
and riding it out like a meteor.

## OLYMPIC STUDIOS (LEFT ON THE FLOOR)

A cache of misfits, stop and start
late night Jagger/Richards out-takes,
canned imperfections, raw
try-outs, a stoned 'Dear Doctor', furred
'Blood Red Wine' 2 a.m. muddied

by off-kilter savvy.
A 'Jumpin' Jack Flash' 1&2
don't meet it square, but miss nailing
the saturnalia with a riff
clean as a shark's grin.

A bootlegger's stock exchange sting,
the numbers go disowned and stay
as a completist's legacy –
a straggly 'You Got The Silver'
cat-licked to numbness by Jagger

as though he'd caught the mouse
and let it go.
A high octane 'Downtown Suzie'
is so tricky its dynamic's
wacky as robo-soldiers

able to shoot round corners.
Hear a floor-crawling 'Sister Morphine'
still half-cooked, its subject messed
on mainlining, Chelsea's own
disingenuous Marianne.

'No Expectations' as a rough
isn't personalised by Brian's
valetudinarian slide,
his spooky figures conjuring
imminent ruin, absent here.

Nights at Barnes, limos parked up
under 1968 rain.
The songs left over are eponymous
reminders of the lost and found
Decca dispossessions that still remain.

## GOING DOWN

Bare torso, pink scarf tied around his head,
Mick dances his shamanic Nijinsky –
*L'Après-midi d'un faune* electrified

by blasting rock in the full-length mirror
at Cheyne Walk. He attacks like a whip,
then draws back, teasing like a pouty rose.

The room gives on the river's shimmered lick,
all Moroccan textiles and purple drapes –
tricked out for an odalisque on majoun,

its Ali Baba glitter themed by hash.
His inamorata's on messy drugs
and cheats on him to score each frozen shot

that sends her crashing lights out on the bed.
A snaky wisteria trails a plait
of festooning reminders down one wall –

shy smoky-blue flowers ruffled into frills.
Mick's a midnight to six studio jinn
lashing a lapsed band's fuddled energies

into coherent jams – they tape the lot –
Ry Cooder's figures inked into the mix
like permanent tattoos, slide artistry

coloured like Rimbaud's vowels in analogue . . .
A miscarriage, a film that's done for real –
Cammell tirading mania on the set,

the band re-train direction, get a nose
for criminality, the underside
of London's skin, the Kray hegemony,

the back end of Portobello, and twist
hard drugs into the wiring, blow the lid
on their mythology and give it blast.

## MARIANNE FAITHFULL (2)

The sixties are a loop in the time-film,
pacifism, pot, a blazing decade
extended like a summer through dog-days
to a mellow shimmer. They've gone away,

the ones who expected to change the world
in velvets, lace, the flower-children who sat
up all night with guitars. They disappeared
or recycled themselves in the brain-fade

of too much acid. All the kaftans, beads
were left behind as though a tribe had faced
extinction, and cleared off into the hills.
You were part of that damaged exodus,

one of the rejects hooked on methadone,
excess, smashing the glass to find yourself
without a face or torso. Through the hole
are glass splinters, a blue pigmented wall.

And then that raw whiskey-burnt voice came through
with 'Broken English', concentrated pain
feeding each song, away back into life,
an affirmation that it could be done,

anger and re-birth redress the balance,
point the way to a continuity
for a blonde Billie Holiday; cracked timbre
evoking in part a Brecht cabaret

singer, someone leaning by a piano,
inhaling on a red-tipped cigarette,
feeling into a sad song and assured
despite the shadow, the plaintive regret.

## STREET FIGHTING MAN

The river's filming 1968
as peripatetic cloud lucks over
at Cheyne Walk; a wobbly cumulus

detaches for the Chelsea Harbour build.
Summer smells of blackcurrant: buddleia
pokes purple tusks around the garden house

where Jagger's pop edge raps 'Street Fighting Man'
against Keith's beating-to-quarters chord riff –
the lyric heat-curling with insolence,

driving a revolution to its feet?
They feel their interactive flow, the power
go deep river with psychic energies,

even the song's unstructured rudiments
hinting at action poetry,
a snarlishly wolf-slinky signature

exhorting life in a rock n' roll band.
The tryout's buzzy like a chocolate fix
kicking in endorphins: the hook has bite

and streetwise savvy at its core.
London's its generative firepower.
They try it folksy, bluesy, whack it rock

and feel the playback hang like flame.
They've hit the moment with their anti-war
vehemence, lifted youth the right way up

to burn a flag and overturn the state . . .
They break, and feel the sticky heat oven,
July forcing the honeysuckle's scent

to gorgeous assault, and the future theirs,
hot for the taking, while the sky chokes up
with amazing sculptural slow-roller clouds.

## THE ROCK & ROLL CIRCUS

Jagger's the dressy spiritus rector –
the whip-hand ringmaster, his act's on cue.
Support's from the arena fire-eaters –

a mega-explosive rock-opera Who,
Townshend's molten windmilling power chords
fulminating like he's plugged into the sun.

John Lennon's skewed maverick Dirty Mac
cobble 'Yer Blues' round Clapton's grilling licks,
Yoko bodybagged into a black sack

at Lennon's feet like a dead artefact.
The cast are a decade older, wear tracks:
their arteries are gummed with sticky plaque.

The Stones come on to a ballsy 'Jack Flash',
long curtained hair, capricious, arrogant,
their yardstick's doing wind-ups in the face,

infamously diffident, couldn't care,
the singer shaking ass like a stripper,
fixing the camera with a cobra's stare.

They slow the tempo, Brian's wolfish slide
bleeds into a jittery epitaph –
'No Expectations' and he's terminal –

his pulse measured in each trembling figure.
They build to a macumba 'Sympathy',
a conga-driven litany to waste –

Mick whip-lashing his body like a snake
sticking its prey, then doing a board-crawl –
125lbs of electrified tissue,

amino acids, salts, Artaudian screams,
his satanic persona turned scary
as though he'd really do it in the street.

## BREAKING UP IS HARD TO DO

Chaos is like a drug-coshed interlude
spent in a Russian airport lounge,
fragmented 68-69

the Stones are harnessed to a Burroughs plot
an undercover intelligence sting
worked like a retro-virus in the blood.

The music deconstructs. A fat red sun
monitors World's End, the King's Road.
London is radio-signalled to explode...

The East End's Mad Frank Mitchell and the Krays,
drivers who network substances,
feeding a hold over the band

and over Brian's stunned vulnerability.
A gun's pulled on him at Redlands,
a snouty Colt butting his frontal lobes...

He's mind-fucked into paranoid jitters,
fumbles Moroccan drums and blows a harp
defiantly on 'You Got the Silver'.

Ry Cooder's brought in for slide tricks.
His bottleneck designs 'Sister Morphine'.
He jams. They tape, and later plagiarize

his eloquence. They're out of it
in the slow penumbral sunset
of a dying decade, a corona

dusting the West, the dark rising
over Olympic studios, its push
working history to continuity...

## THE BIG SPLASH

A busted spine-strafed Penguin Brighton Rock
sits face up in the Redlands spill
of loony clutter – Keith's rehab centre –

one nervy day in 1968,
the band convening, while Ry Cooder's slide,
an open G tuning (five strings only)

morphs 'Sister Morphine' with an eerie tweak
of impetuous eloquence.
A brandy-wiped, redundant Brian Jones,

sits nonplussed, eye-bagged on the red sofa,
too uncoordinated to pick chords.
The clouds are origami postcard stuff

Greene might have eyed when writing *Brighton Rock*.
Brian's hysteria's like fizz shaken up,
the cork popped on the bottle by arrest,

his court case imminent, he starts to blow
in fuming paranoid snips, lashes out
at Jagger's bitchy, bee-stung flippancy,

picks up a knife and runs out to the lawn,
screaming he'll kill himself, bolts for the moat,
bleached hair tousled and flying burnt pink vents,

his rage proportionate to the green thrash
he makes in arcing through the scummed veneer,
frog-kicking as he spraddles in the slime,

a wheezing upended amphibian,
boots wedged in Jagger's palms, wrenched out face down,
shocked but still kicking, like a giant pike

pulled from the weedy murk and cursed by Mick
for dirtying his hands – his velvet suit –
his temper shouting there's no going back.

## MEMO FROM TURNER

A psychosexual lab at Powis Square,
outside, offset, Keith Richards mits
his faux leopard-skin steering-wheel,
fogged out by smoke inside his car,
he beats time like he raps guitar,
jealousy knotted in his fist

at Jagger's boss-cat sexual fest
with his trashy sleep around:
Pallenberg doing it for real
with Mick's reactor-like libido
hot as the Amazon basin, steamy
as a flickery liana.

The shooting frames the 60s live,
the studied rock star shadowed by gofers,
Kray-links, bespoke gangsters in spotty ties,
East End yardies snowed on cocaine,
dodgy low lifers working for the Stones
like sticky bees around a hive.

The new aristos in their ecosphere,
Mick's hair is swishy Elvis-black,
his sexuality so epicene
he dissolves boundaries, swims through the two girls
and out again, a hologram
with a man's front, a woman's back.

The gangster taking refuge in the den
stays quizzical and angular,
rough edges teething like a saw.
He's straight, but colours like Pernod
with orange juice, resists, but spikes
the cocktail with a drinking straw.

Mick calls the shots. A magus holding court,
his slippery epigone at his feet.
A decade muddies like a Rolls-Royce hub,
violence integrated into its nerves.
His lips are glossed, his manicure complete.
He struts his hi-stuff through the druggy fort.

Whose execution is prepared by this?
We don't see clearly who's inside the car
slicing a line through 1968;
the limo bashed away from a near square,
the ritual victim silenced, and its thrust
picking up speed across Notting Hill Gate.

## DEATH BY WATER – BRIAN JONES

High summer, and the squat oaks chase a breeze
to sibilant, wind-chimish expiry.
He's countrified: foppish and floppily

reviewing water and its quizzed print-out
of flurried tremolos. All day the pool
goes goose-pimply under slow, churning cloud.

Water's the skin he breaks to know himself
weightlessly free, a soluble figure
dissolving down moods into buoyancy.

The scare's inside him as conspiracy:
the builders talk death threats into his nerves
as an insidious telepathy.

He's sighted as a sacrificial claim,
a generation's ritual offering
to its excesses: sex and drugs and fame.

His mind's crowded with restorative schemes,
new sounds, new band: he stretches in the sun
and for a moment sees the future blonde.

They're back again, the adversarial ones
with their bad frequencies. They stand around,
freeloaders waiting on their time to kill.

It's evening, and a lazy rose subsides,
volute tucked into red volute, the flower
aware of its peculiar entropy.

His hair's turned bleached nasturtium. He's afraid.
His in-head theatre associates death
with some involuntary pact he's made.

He dives, and smells the water's chlorine slack,
his killers roughing him: one detaches
and fastens like a double to his back.

They twin that way, one body and two skins
in a coital thrash, a stranglehold,
while others muscle in to the attack.

The floodlit water kicks. He stays on down
without resistance, turns a limp 3D,
his killers scattering divergent ways.

# PART 3

# THE MICK TAYLOR YEARS: 1969–1974

## MICK TAYLOR

Arrives like a sweet pea, dead on time,
9 June 1969
summer coaxing sweet peas to intertwine,
a pink, a blue and red
stringy as vine.
He's gangly, thin-waisted like a decade
measuring 28"
closing like Hannibal's troops on Hyde Park,
London itself rolled into a collective joint,
a fuming heady volcano
blazing with hot euphoria,
the Stones materialising like genie
out of a psychotropic mirage.
Taylor's a tempo primo
virtuoso,
his blues figures texturing shape
to 'Brown Sugar', his clean palette
comprising primaries, colours
picked up by rhythm and remixed
as urgent, feral arpeggios.
He's backgrounded, a chiaroscuro slot
in the Grand Guignol's arena,
a taciturn, undervalued maestro
at sculptural licks, denied credits
as a riff-catalyst, then hooking up
to a smack habit, heroin
as the invasive leveller,
the time-killer feeding receptor-sites
with empty plateaus, flat ennui.
He stays there, five years in that frigid space
like someone dug into the moon
inside a moon-rock shelter, then walks out
as a blues nomad, cuts solo
and disappears, sucked into a black hole.

## WINTER

Ice sparkles underfoot as diamond sprays.
November, Stargroves, and a jay's
ululating apache scream

whoops from a humpbacked, rimed Cromwellian oak
roots sucking mucky history.
The band arrive in swishy knee-length furs

blowing on knuckles like a horn.
The pile is woody. 16<sup>th</sup>-century halls
roomy with blocks of unused time

awaiting retrieval. They stomp indoors
Englished by their eccentric pedigree,
ballsy on tea laced with Feret Branca,

January in their veins, a new decade
coded in a snowflake's rhomboid,
a solitary pre-fall flutter

of parachuting molecules.
Mick Taylor's amp's cubed into the fireplace
for 'Sway', his molten solo heals

the edgy tensions in the room.
Mick humps into 'Cocksucker Blues',
lyrics a cottage graffito's

crude slash of queeny energies.
The Human Riff's too comatose to pick.
Bill eyes a message written on the floor.

Their sound is dirtier like temper stored
six months before it blows, a raw weather
expression patterned from the bay window

by Charlie's skins, while outside convoyed clouds
stack over Newbury and the slack air's
shaken like a domed paperweight with snow.

## REHEARSALS

A feedback turbo-whine, a Boeing roar,
their stop and start tuning's so dissonant
from an irascible plastic guitar

creating hangar noise on soundstage four,
it's like an airbase moved into the hall
with all its high-pitched engine repertoire...

Gram Parsons lines snow on an album sleeve,
a Lonnie Mack record, and fired up now
leans into the re-energised assault.

The rhythm's tight: they blast 'Little Queenie'
through twenty-five Ampeg amps, strut the song
to an impersonally self-coloured jaunt.

Jagger's sore throat gives tonsils to 'I'm Free',
his rose-coloured shirt, open to the waist,
moves with him like a wind-gathered peony.

They trainrush 'Satisfaction', muscle it
to mock-heroics, disabuse the take,
then wrong-tune 'Let It Bleed' to a dead end.

They're seriously redemptive, red-lighting
their Honky Tonk persona, working tight
at managing a phallocentric riff.

A bottle of Wild Turkey oils their licks,
loosens dimensions, and the band comes right,
mainlining power like they might explode.

They down guitars. Jagger's pink velvet cap's
a patisserie embonpoint, put on slouch
as a token they're through and top cherry.

## THE STONES IN THE PARK

A spinach-green armoured van remonstrates
at every jostle, squat chassis
rocked to a tidal swell by hands

stalling its square-faced amphibian's crawl
in jerky segues through the park.
The heat's a jacuzzi; the crowd tailbacks

into a magnetic hologram.
The light's stripped of its ozone defences.
Hell's Angels do their janitorials

with sunstroke casualties. The band
don't come up right, the rhythm's out,
arrhythmia dominating the beat

that's scrambled to unrehearsed register.
Jagger's postured Mr Fish mini-dress
feeds a dervish androgyny

into the mile-deep swarm, trees snaggily
rippling with branch-forked onlookers
got high from ceremonials

and marijuana licks.
The music's raw and undercooked,
de-centred by miragey déjà vu,

they've all known this before when dead,
a packed assembly in the underworld,
instructors waiting on a bridge.

They play for Brian's absence in the park,
and how he's amongst the white butterflies
released like petals on the wind.

The music drags. They keep the lost one near
in heat-shimmer as an obituarised
dispersal, lifted up towards the sun.

## SUGAR AND SPICE

Time's like a perky orange
to be squeezed of its info,
decoded like DNA junk
for gene referentials:
each generation
hacks at the neural tree,
gets thrown out of the precinct –
Woodstock, Haight-Ashbury
or the Stones in the park
gunning tracks at the trees
royal oaks stationed
with scorched knotty antlers
standing like custodians
of the urban migration
to a grilled Hyde Park.
Jagger in a white dress
de-genders machismo
fellates the mike
struts in stripper's heels...
Cut the age from its skin,
the tissue reassembles
the track marks rubbed clean
like disinformation;
the 1960s soup
infected by toxins,
ideals blown out like tyres
on heavy metal roads;
but for a summer afternoon
belief's mapped in the music,
a wonky 'Honky Tonk Woman'
scrambled like garage,
most of London emptied
by the gravitational pull

to Jagger's sassy preening
at a celebratory memorial,
Brian Jones dead, and time standing still,
his killers in the crowd?
watching the trashy blissed out
rocky solar ritual.

## HYDE PARK 5 JULY 1969

A sudden explosive roar went up, like the park had been vacuumed into space, as the Stones, surrounded by security, were hustled towards the stage; diminutive, long-haired figures, stuck at the end of a decade, attempting still to alter time by recreating the bad boy music and attitude with which they had begun the sixties.

From his wasted look, Keith Richards was out of it on drugs, and the band were débuting their 19-year-old guitarist, Mick Taylor, chosen to replace Brian Jones. Mick Jagger was wearing what looked like a white ruffled mini-dress, over white jeans, as the ultimate personification of stick-skinny androgyny, confrontationally, facing up to the massively compacted crowd.

Jagger approached the mic, sluttishly, book in hand, and controversially arrogant in his preening conceit. 'Cool it. Fucking shut up. I wanna read a poem for Brian,' he asserted, as he tried at the third attempt to get some sort of focused attention from the crowd. Most didn't know what Jagger was reading so unconvincingly: 'Peace, peace, he is not dead, he doth not sleep/ He hath awakened from the dream of life,' the affected drawl flattening the words, and relieved only by the band launching into a raunchy 'I'm Yours She's Mine', in an origami cloud of white butterflies released as a symbolic tribute to the dead Brian Jones.

The band, right from the start, struggled to keep time behind the energised, white-frocked singer, throwing contorted pelvic shapes across a stage overloaded with security and the Stones' personal entourage. What was immediately apparent was the virtuosic facility of the new member, Mick Taylor's, playing, as he arrestingly piloted the sound with colourful licks that compensated for Keith Richards' narcoleptic chords and the band scorched into 'Jumping Jack Flash', with only Charlie Watts nailing down a time, which the others ineptly struggled to keep in the heat.

The Stones began to get it together, for the first time, with the slow Blues of 'No Expectations', the guitars meshing in what was clearly an elegiac pointer to their dead colleague whose life had run out so early. For the first time that afternoon, Brian Jones's presence came alive physically, in the music and in the park, the band's empathy with loss cooking a raw Blues that had them sound mean, riffy, and right on the case. Ten minutes later, the Stones repeated their slow moody success with a slumped, degenerate slide-trawl through Robert Johnson's 'Love In Vain', with the blond teenage Mick Taylor sounding like a maestro, silencing the crowd with his wounded chords like he was creating a tangible heartbeat for Brian Jones's absent body.

The Stones completely lost it on 'Satisfaction', the guitars jumping out of tune, and Mick Jagger, free of his dress now on account of the heat, was stripped to a white T-shirt and jeans as the phallic interpreter of chords, a Rock shaman making up for the band's laconic performance through a body projected across the stage as a frenetic white diagram, throwing menacing shapes at the crowd.

The Stones didn't do themselves any favours with their new number, 'Honky Tonk Woman'. Announced as a song about a bar-room queen in Texas and as their next single, the two guitars sounded right out of tune, and the delivery altogether lacked edge, as the Stones struggled hard with the heat and the attempt to avoid flagrant self-parody.

The entire park seemed to represent late-sixties revivalists hanging in uncritically on the Stones as they surged into an angry 'Street Fighting Man', the guitars ringing noisily with Keith Richards' open tunings for rhythm parts, and Jagger projecting his sensational dynamic across the stage, and actually meaning it this time, in a voice that seemed to speak for an entire generation's presumptive anger with drug raids, the Vietnam war, increased police power, and the consolidated social reprisals issued by an older generation on a youth liberated into sex, drugs and Rock 'n' Roll. For once in the afternoon the band was immersed in the music, the rhythm section perfect in their timing, the guitars confrontationally angry, and the insurgent vocal nailing the song for real.

It wasn't the raw, subversive Stones of the primitive Scene, throwing R&B shapes off the club's sweaty black walls, but the song was a temporary absorbent that got above band posturing for real. The Stones got back together fully on 'Street Fighting Man', as a counter-culture slap at the authorities, from Whitehall to the White House, with Richards prominently holding the lip of the stage and playing to kill, tight as a central-marker line. The whole park rose in response, an affirmative sea of salutatory arms, as the Stones succeeded in scorching a gateway to revolution for the proletariat against the criminally systemised establishment.

The giant stage was decorated with palm trees and gantries, creating the effect of a tropical island in the middle of Hyde Park, with the popocracy and their chic entourage isolated there like passengers on a cruise ship, staring out at the heat-slicked turquoise Caribbean.

The sun-bleached crowd was by now growing restless as Mick Jagger made way to introduce Ginger Johnson's African drummers, all dressed in tribal costumes, for support on 'Sympathy for the Devil', the unforgettable lead *Beggars Banquet* album song that cast Jagger in the disruptive persona of Lucifer and the band as confirmed satanic antagonists to the authorities.

The African drum intro to the song was a chaotic primal bongo, before the band came in casually, without conviction, and Jagger chased the number hard, without ever properly integrating his vocals into the choppy beat, stretching the lyric, crawling antagonistically to the lip of the stage, just out of finger-reach of the crushed fangirls, who were trying to get a handhold and drag him under. For a timeless moment, the entire park was focused on his expressively eroticised dance steps, before the band were quite suddenly gone to an applause that vacuumed West London into a vast shattering.

## MIAMI 1969

Black marble bath tubs at the Colonnades.
The wind's a sonic frisbee stripping palms
        in cold
            so zero it's solid.
The dawn when it fires up is red and gold.

They're eight hours late. Palm Beach is quagmired mud.
Their helicopter bops into the squall,
        hangs dead,
        buggishly oscillates,
its position lights twinkle green and red.

The crowds are glued to gelled mud underfoot,
like survivors of a catastrophe
        who wait
        for air-freighted relief
and just hang on, although its growing late.

The band are jacketed against the cold
and tune defiantly into the wind.
        Drums crash
        as extempore intro
to a choppily skewed 'Jumpin' Jack Flash'.

They work to hold a centre in the storm,
strings breaking in hurt fingers and the sound
      wonky,
        inverting on itself
like some debilitated energy.

Richards in his red rhinestoned Nudie shirt
builds bluesy aural plateaus round 'Stray Cat'
        guitar
        talking a deep south dialect,
body leaned into a spotlight's blue star.

Some freakies stay angled in sleeping-bags,
toke joints, and reconnect with a love-in
        gone bad
           unity deconstructed,
or dance to `Live with Me' but remain sad.

It's 'Satisfaction' builds to overload,
reverberated bass strings, percussion
        so loud
           it's like a landslide's kick-in speed
grooving a mountain through low-flying cloud.

'Street Fighting Man' is so urgent it fries
inside the diaphragm, its directives
        that scorched
           it has the strained crowd pack
as though the rain-gunned Raceway had been torched.

They encore 'Honky Tonk Woman', squeal dead
on the hard raunchy closer. Jagger flings
        a high arc
           basket of red rose petals
over the near ones stomping in the dark.

## ROLL CALL (1969)

A stone robber's roost in Laurel Canyon –
the valley throbbing with eucalyptus,
oaks pushing weight into a sky
dissolving blue in cloudy blue,
for clear November – the days wide as America

with slow clouds paddling in the swimming pool.
The mortuary-sized black refrigerator's
stocked with beer courtesy
of Stephen Stills.
Stone walls, stone fireplace, rustic hick.
Belmont, Steckler and Sandison

hang out as Stetsoned auxiliaries
boots up in the living room.
A Rodeo tailored Gram Parsons rakes
a Crowley Tarot pack on the sofa,
ponders the Hanging Man, then reads
a spiky letter from his father,

needy as a desert cactus.
Mick Taylor tunes in the rehearsal room,
deadheading chords so perfectly
the sound's picked up telepathically
on air-waves in Mississippi
all over the Delta.

A cougar tooth ringed in his right ear lobe,
Keith necks a bottle with gapped teeth
and does a narcoleptic freeze
on discourse, pulls his black shades down
over a death-mask, lifts a spoon
and twinkles like a hologram.

The Stones are outlaws in the hills,
gunning to storm the USA,
but for the moment seem Dionysian
leopards trooping after the fawn
through redwood canyons, buckskin gods
joined in their concupiscent play.

## THE L.A. FORUM '69

Jagger's Nijinsky's act-alike
a daemonic chimera
melding *L'Après-midi d'un faune*
on understudied Tina Turner,
King Bitch dressed by Ossie Clark
in black off-the-shoulder,
rhinestone-belted gaucho pants
and a knee-length floaty scarf
like Isadora Duncan.
Richards' transparent guitar
kills from its infrastructure:
the virtuoso Mick Taylor
writing italics in a riff
as a detailed figure.
America's their money-trail,
jostled by weirdos, dissenters,
Black Panthers, feral
gun-threatening activists, they phrase
the lot in 'Gimme Shelter',
invoke a conspiratorial
sister from out the breaking storm,
to surf the thunder to its core.
They're hardwired to dystopian
uprisings, Jagger face-slapping
the mike like an antagonist,
their power lined to a continent
that moves with them like beginnings
of a stormy-blue tidal wave
growing from swell to a curved wall
collapsing in on final ends
in the consensus of a shattered roar.

## BOWING OUT

Reverse in slow-motion
like an actress bowing out
Mick slews the wicker basket
crammed with red rose petals
colour of Châteauneuf-du-Pape
in a scarlet parabola
over the black Gossard C-cups
shirtless in the front row
Keith's amps like a car tunnel
right up to sonic blow-out
guitar saddled on the hip
like a lean gunslinger
directing 'Street Fighting Man'
low from the groin
as gonadal thunder
under scorching orange lights
at Madison Square Garden
the pulse jammed on danger
like a car horn stuck,
wailing from the air-bag
in a black finned crash,
the upfront with tinnitus
injected by the bash,
Mick doing his Nijinsky
behind a red storm
of migrating scallops
in a suspended arc
the band unplugging
and bolting for their lives,
demythicised in that instant
of panicky dispersal,
cheetah it backstage
out to a tanky limo,

the bodyguards like bulwarks
cemented to a dock,
the car blinding in zigzags
of rage without a muffler
irascibly hairpinning
a right-angled block.

## JAGGER'S DANCE STEPS

At the Crawdaddy, Eel Pie, Ham's Yard, Ricky Tick,
he's gauchely disingenuous,
Presley-twitchy, bird-boned, jejeune
in hipsters and a thistle-grey
lambswool crew-neck from Cecil Gee,
mouth like he's biting on a Granny Smith's
a fist-sized, acidy green
ellipsoid.
He's cross-legged, like he's bondage-tied,
invents himself from awkward tries
to a draggy autonomy
a bona fide Nancy act,
legs knotted like the upfront crowd
crushed by a shock-waved tsunami
against the stage; hysteria
slapping the walls like rowdy surf.
His hands snap out disjointedly,
his head keeps rhythm; on stubbed toes
he minces like he's foot-bandaged,
then flips into gestural striptease,
fingers splayed out, and channelling
deep Mississippi in his raw
re-hash of it beside the Thames.
Years later he's androgyny,
a stick-insect with floaty scarves,
sweating a thunderstorm on stage, a monsoon
leaving the boards peppered with holes
from a leather belt thrashed so hard
the grain looks pocked by stilettos.
He's 125 lbs of hot explosive
rephrasing every black dance act
by upping the ante,
streamlining payload for the max

burn-up, fuelled by delirious thrust,
like a surfer riding a tidal wave
into a coastal town and out
on shattered rebound to a violent sea.

## NASTY HABITS: MICK TAYLOR'S ROLLING STONES

In the year preceding Brian Jones's murder at Cotchford Farm, Sussex, on 2 July 1969, having been ignominiously fired by the Rolling Stones on 9 June, ostensibly for an assumed indifference to the band's directional thrust, and equally due to increasingly dysfunctional behaviour that had him diffidently avoid studio sessions, as well as come up for drug convictions making it impossible for him to tour the States, the Stones were busy reclaiming their raw blues origins after a period of being drenched in the King's Road psychedelics as a psychoactive aura that put a lysergic rainbow over Chelsea's World's End.

Off the road for nearly three years, and losing chart credibility with their dip into psychedelia *Their Satanic Majesties Request*, the band had in 1968 roughed it back to roots with the driving blues aggro fuelling 'Jumpin' Jack Flash,' as a smash hit, and the Thames muddy trawl through blues and folk rock that inspired *Beggar's Banquet* with its dystopian epic 'Sympathy for the Devil', a slice of leftfield occult politics that while it launches global terrorism as a theme, still smells of the Thames, the tidal reach at sticky Cheyne Walk down to the reconstructed ergonomics of Chelsea Harbour.

Somewhere tied into the Brian Jones redundancy, the dandy in self-imposed exile from the *Let It Bleed* sessions at Olympic, this pretty boy arrives, a 21-year old guitar maestro hardwired to extravagant virtuoso blues riffs, having played with the seminal John Mayall and the Bluesbreakers, a romantic melodist with a fluency that had a clear Andalusian-sounding start on any guitarist of his generation. An idealist born in Hertfordshire on 17 January 1948, his long blond wavy hair partially obscuring faded-denim blue eyes, his attitude appeared so refreshingly substance-free that he didn't initially seem to fit with the band's increasingly degenerative look via Jagger and Richards' Quorum, Hung On You, Granny Takes A Trip and Chelsea Antiques Market clothes grabs as the visual counterparts of increasingly customised mind-altering psychoactives.

Mick Taylor's Stones-skinny 28" waist, maybe 140lbs max, the turned-up nose lending an androgynous profile, reputably vegetarian, acutely shy, but so constructively authoritarian in his playing, it's like he's got blues genes, riffy chromosomes and a textural facility to colour that leaves Richards raw, loud and seriously compromised is instantly great. What he remembers of his first rehearsal with the band, after being phoned by Jagger, literally out of the blue, was that they were 'really ragged. I thought how do these guys make such great records when they're so sloppy and spontaneous? But it was because they had this great chemistry.'

That was in 1969, terminal hipster sixties, an idealistic, sexually ambiguous liberated, fashion, music and drugs drenched decade going into warp-drive – the amalgamated substrate of mod and period revival hippy, blues and psychedelia becoming power-pointed into the Stones as R&B aggressors with the look of bandit cross-dressing delinquents. Intro Mick Taylor: the Stones' last kamikaze live gig was Athens, 17 April 1967, and it was Brian Jones's penultimate live performance with the band; his last, wearing girlie pink lipstick and dressed in a purple velvet jacket, being a jittery, caked appearance at the Rock & Roll Circus jamboree filmed over three days, 10-12 December 1968, at InterTel studios in Wembley, where Brian bled inimitable slide into 'No Expectations,' almost as a prescient obituary; a deeply elegiac confessional riff that was his last with the Stones.

And Mick, Mick Taylor, (the first choice after Eric Clapton refused), his sumptuously fluent playing on *Bare Wires* (1968) with John Mayall's Bluesbreakers posting helium into arabesque figures, elevating blues into ethereal arpeggios, most of it self-taught from listening to B.B. King records, seemed to have it all with effortless facility.

It wasn't even that he was a Stones fan – he'd picked up on the raw energies of the aggressive 'Street Fighting Man' from *Beggar's Banquet*, but he didn't really rate Keith Richards' overloud maverick playing or the band's crude lack of technical proficiency. Mick was exoplanetary.

On 30 May 1969 – hawthorn flowering time – Mick Taylor, who'd recently left the Bluesbreakers, was completely thrown to get an importuning call from Mick Jagger asking him to join the Stones on the *Let It Bleed* recording sessions, exactly nine days before the radically destabilised Brian Jones was fired by the Stones as a drug habituated casualty, too physically debilitated and dependent to join the Stones' upcoming American stadium tour that for the first time targeted stadia and was due to net the band a million dollars as bankable incentive.

According to Mick Taylor, his being contacted by the Stones initially implied session work, and most certainly not band membership. 'I was invited to do a session with the Stones, it puzzled me. I had never met Mick Jagger in my life and here he was phoning me. I went down and played on some tracks and thought little more about it. Then they asked me if I wanted to be a Stone. I was amazed Brian Jones was leaving, I was told. The first song I worked on was called "Live With Me", very appropriately named because once I joined the Stones, it was like living with a family for the next five or six years. It was an interesting session, actually, because they were putting the finishing touches on *Let It Bleed* and the first track I played on was "Live With Me". We did that live, and the second thing I did was I overdubbed my guitar part on "Honky Tonk Woman".'

While the crunching buccaneering riffs on 'Honky Tonk Woman' were created by Keith Richards' idiosyncratic open-G tuning, a technique copied in part from Ry Cooder, Taylor's magical colouring was to contribute a country-style inflection on the rock licks between the polysexual bar room verses phrased by Jagger, not only with misogynistic contempt, but also with disrespect for all preconceived gender frontiers. While it's the vocal attitude carries the song, Taylor's apprentice decoration transforms the basic rock riff into layered artistry, as though his contribution can't be learnt, it can't be bettered either, and like all his work you don't go higher.

Mick Taylor's never told his Stones story or how he inwardly reacted to being the band's choice at a time when he was simply a session musician, his potential hardly realised, and when it was assumed in the industry that Eric Clapton would substitute for Brian Jones' chaotically imploded talents. But Clapton would have majorly reduced Richards' playing, would have overshadowed it completely with his stratospheric riffs that also hacked into cerebrally tooled psychedelia with a purchase that only Jimi Hendrix amongst his contemporaries could manage.

Taylor proved to be by the Stones' own admission too musically proficient for their playing, his undemonstrative stage presence and total absorption into the music being in strict contrast to the hyperactive Jagger/Richards interactive showman strut with demands for optimal audience attention. While Mick Taylor looked cute, wore the right clothes and eye makeup, and was the prettiest Stone, he mostly on live footage appears dissociated, diminished by the Jagger/Richards ostentatious effrontery and wanting almost to dematerialise into the music at the expense of image. For five crucial years Mick Taylor's propulsive, maverick, virtuous riff-driven, almost gypsified playing, both in the studio and live, piloted a bandit rock style, so blues colourfully defined and redefined on *Sticky Fingers* and *Exile On Main Street* that his playing formulated a sound so inimitably cool that it remains to purists the ultimate Stones decadent genre, never bettered and instantly identifiable with the period 1969-1972 in which they peaked musically with arrogant conquistadorial firepower.

Of that period in a recent Mojo interview, January 2012, Mick Taylor commented: 'The first thing I ever played with the Stones was "Live With Me" (on *Let It Bleed*) and, looking back, that turned out to be a prophetic song, because we all ended up living together. Those years in the mid-'70s were manic. We were either in the studio or on the road, always doing something. You neglect other parts of your life, but I don't think it matters when you're in your youth, as we were. You should be doing what you're best at: making music and having fun and making some money – and we managed all three in that period.'

Taylor joined the Stones provisionally on a salary of £150 a week, before becoming an integrated band member by the close of the 1969 US tour; but neither celebrity nor money appear to have been motivations to Taylor's outwardly submerged personality. It's rumoured in Stones apocrypha that Richards was seminal to getting Taylor habituated to heroin, a serious drug problem that seems according to Taylor to have continued well into the nineties. His own ambiguity on his habit suggests he may already have been a recreational user at the time he joined the band, not uncommon amongst sixties musicians to whom drugs were readily available currency.

At the photo call in Hyde Park on 13 June 1969 when the band announced Mick Taylor as the replacement for Brain Jones, Taylor isn't looking at the camera, his eyes are downturned shyly, and he's dressed casually in an ivory cotton jacket, a lipstick red and cornflower blue tee-shirt, and black trousers, a throwback to structurally casual Mod, rather than the hippy or fusion period revival Granny Takes A Trip look adopted by the majority of the sun-drenched half a million crowd saturating the park from every angle. The crowd were predominantly stoned, navigating altered states under the dense oak and plane trees, throwing colours, and Mick Taylor's this rogue gene under intense critical scrutiny, but too stunningly proficient a player to be nervous. Already he's incorporated not only into the Stones' organism, but enhances the sound by stratospheric blues licks:
cyan
cobalt
turquoise
laps lazuli

ultramarine
navy blue
foggy blue
the band lacked in their palette before. On 30 June 1969, Taylor had contributed to the exhaustive Olympic session for 'I Don't Know Why', an agonized Stevie Wonder, Paul Riser, Don Hunter and Lula Hardaway-written song that never made it on to *Let It Bleed* to which he supplied elegiac licks that sound like chords pinched to the sonic equivalent of grief. Mick Taylor contributed significantly to two other songs recorded at the time, 'Jiving Sister Fanny' and the scorching 'Going Down', an upbeat driver featuring Rocky Dijon on bass, Bobby Keyes on sax and Bill Plummer on bass, the number fuelled by the full on firepower of Taylor's urgently menacing guitar. Taylor was given a song writing credit for 'Going Down', but the number was considered too inchoate for inclusion on *Let It Bleed*, and instead ended up on *Metamorphosis* (1971), a compendium of sixties outtakes and demos considered by their record company worthy of reappraisal for Stones' completists.

Taylor, as the undecoded black box of Stones' secret data, during arguably their most decadent, rootsy period – 1969-1973 – has told us little or nothing of those expressly compressed times in which his individual playing won into a bandit-riffy, smacked out, river muddy rocky blues, the live personification of it captured on *Get Yer Ya Yahs Out* from Madison Square, December 1969. He's there too on the seminal Stones bootleg *Liver Than You'll Ever Be*, an audience recording from the Oakland Colliseum, 9 November 1969, 2nd show, recorded on a Seheiser 805 shotgun microphone and a Uher 4000 reel-to-reel tape recorder, and released in December 1969 on the Lurch label, the recording produced and manufactured by Trade Mark of Quality TMOQ to ensure professional grading and the primal depth of the illegally grabbed recording that finds Taylor and the band at their most optimally primitive and nasty. What's immediately signature into this recording is Taylor's shattering virtuoso facility as a standout from the Stones' raw drenched power as loud rampaging desperados burning a drug-fuelled trail across a lysergically hallucinated turbulent USA.

The 2010 expanded reissue of *Exile on Main Street*, with 10 previously unreleased tracks, despite the abundance of unofficially released outtakes over the years, provides further instance of Taylor's superlative gift as virtuoso expressionist, particularly on tracks like 'So Divine (Aladdin's Story)'; and an even more comprehensive assemblage of his Stones' duration is to be found on *The Rolling Stones Genuine Black Box Volume 3 1969–74* – the Taylor years – that throws up blue diamonds like 'Hillside Blues' and 'Travelling Man' – six minutes of sensational blues rock flourishes on Taylor's part, recorded in October 1970 at Olympic, as a live-in-the-studio energised declaration of nasty habits.

Mick Taylor's reluctance to detail the seminal role he played in consolidating the Stones' transitioning early seventies vitally bankable bad boys brand is somehow typical of the habituated off-world personality that led to his incredulously walking out on the Stones at a time when his virtuoso playing was at its peak, and inseparably incorporated into the Stones' virulent tropical diseases sound, as a focus lost on his significantly less talented replacement Ronnie Wood. Taylor abdicated from unique riffdom: if his fired predecessor Brian Jones was an eclectic instrumental maverick, who wasn't physically up to the demands of playing heavy stadium rock, then Mick Taylor directed his arpeggios with the same dynamic authority as Eric Clapton, Jimmy Page and the unparalleled licks-voodooist Jimi Hendrix. What Taylor seems to have lacked was any motivation to form an individual image within the band, preferring instead to be incorporated into the sound rather than a projected personality.

Nor it seems was Taylor's essentially off-message introspection any deliberate attempt on his part to cultivate exclusive mystique, rather it seems his innate shyness kept him unattached to the celebrity so consciously brokered by Jagger and Richards, and self-consciously backgrounded from PR despite his prettiness and enviable focus as the Stones' lead guitarist. Taylor, despite the centrality of his role both live and in the studio on *Let It Bleed, Get Yer Ya Yahs Out, Sticky Fingers, Exile on Main Street, Goat's Head Soup* and *It's Only Rock 'n' Roll* remains the inaccessible enigmatic Stone, a superlative player in all the right patterned shirts, who appeared elusively exoplanetary or un-Stoned in commitment to the idea of the band as early seventies family.

## SATAN RISING (ALTAMONT 1969)

At Altamont the crowds are packed like wheat
jostled by wind, expansive hippie wave
on repossessing wave. The racetrack's burnt:
a chassis litters debris on the grass.

December's shot with diamond: pink-sleeved fog.
Hell's Angels in their chaptered solidarity
have centre-staged their leather brotherhood,
chains, boots and pool cues, a high-handled hog...

They're unsanctioned security to bands,
a lawless, pro-Manson fraternity
boasting perverse insignias: arson,
gang-rape, kidnap and bestiality...

The crowds are drug-resistant to the cold,
some naked, as they shoulder their own heat
in dazed anticipation of the Stones,
red stage lights strobing into blue and gold,

the many a global anatomy
supported by three-hundred-thousand feet.
The Angels lead the band like criminals
on to a darkened stage and thuggishly

compete for spotlight, as custodians.
When Jagger comes on in a satin cape
he works for upfront space: the speakers roar
as though an aircraft throttled into lift...

It's 'Gimme Shelter' launched into the dark
on tetchily discordant chords provokes
a vicious flail of pool cues from the stage,
a random aimed leather-muscled attack,

sticks finding targets in the tranced-out pack.
The singer minces to a stop and start
striptease dynamic in howling reverb,
slewing into his wide-eyed satanic

embodiment, 'A man of wealth and taste,'
the sneering cookie moving in on kill,
strutting defiance, as the samba beat
translates itself into blood ritual.

Someone is knifed and trampled and the crowd
opens and closes, raising bloody fists
in protest, as the steaming Hell's Angels
hack in again – boots chinning where they hit.

The music holds up: riffs a rockier
mean cat blues crescendo, uncompromised
and in between the nervous pauses gunned
like ECT into fazed pacifists

witnessing murder with a butcher's knife.
The band coax psycho-jitters as they plot
the Boston strangler's serial appetite
to noose a stocking round a jugular,

the notes so chilly they twist in the nerves
like acupuncture pins, the climax gripped
like sacrificial death, the sixties dead,
ripped up by punishing guitars . . .

The Angels churn in, and the band take flight,
chasing from one decade into the next,
their helicopter lifting urgently
over the arena into black night.

## MYTH

Backstage eyeliner's
morphed into
snake's tails

a sax honks its pedigree
bluesman's wail.
A tequila colours

to cloudy definition
red into orange
like a parrot tulip.

A guitar's brouhaha
fine-tunes a howl
like a hyena.

A make-up artist
works tone from a palette
like Francis Bacon

doing a blue.
The myth's the Dionysian
rite of regeneration,

blood on their trail
and a leopard skin coat
left behind in woods

at Tuscaloosa.
They rebirth their dead
through shape-shifting blues,

Meredith Hunter
and fugitive Brian Jones:
the gateway to power

leaving no option,
but to burn up a continent
down south to Virginia.

## DEATH

Comes up like a bruise
on the fruit's underside; downy red peach
topped by gravity.

Mick crawls on all fours
into a spotlight's hot
tiger's eye coloured

like an Aztec sacrifice,
beats the stage with studs cobbled
to a King's Road belt,

kneels like a target –
a miked preying mantis
choreographing mania

to sophomore corybants
mouths hinged open
with glossolalia...

He's every inch a target
for a gunman's .38
polished Smith and Wesson

chamfered bullet
in orange tails and wacky
Uncle Sam top hat.

A Hell's Angel sights him
freezes on the squeeze,
lets the moment go:

'who killed the Kennedys?'
accusatively spat
out like execration

into the squally hall
Mick glowing like a peach skin
escaped its bruising fall.

## SATURNALIA (1970)

A limo cortège musters into town,
 buffed chrome and polished hoods,
a mobile occult lodge, bad blood
 profiled with chemicals, they cook
        a mood now up, now down,
        pre-warned a contract's taken out

to liquidate the Glimmer twins on stage.
 Tequila's like an Aztec
sacrifice, frying raw tracks
 across the liver, gummy scent
        Richards shares with his entourage
        the empty wrested from the car

to shatter as a bright impacted star.
 He's a rock legionnaire
back from the badlands with a flair
 for H, an intravenous binge
        having him sleepwalk out so far
        he's a dead planet invader

a revenant engaged in jujitsu
 with a Gibson guitar.
Jagger's the sun-up avatar
 louche bacchante with a .38
        he gangsters in his coat, its blue
        precisional snout like a Dobermann's.

Their hotel floor's a pansexual coven
 convened by a weird coterie
feeding like a sea anemone
 on the band's undertow.
            They talk of Chelsea, London rain,
                girls in their strappy bijou shoes,

the King's Road and *trompe l'oeil* collectibles.
 They're Philadelphia and its war
on stage pumping 'Brown Sugar'
 to high octane energy
            the riot gunned by decibels
                and a pig's liver thrown on to the stage.

They hex a continent by playing mean
 Crowley's aficionados
combining caviar with snow,
 faces frozen like petroglyphs
            presided over by a queen
                in cerise satin. When they theme it slow

they're sad like rain falling through a deep wood
 at night, a melancholy
refrain invasively
 speaking of loss and common pain
            and that deep river in the blood
                putting a narrative to every hurt.

Down South they recruit a seraglio
 like arranging a cornucopia
for a flesh-eating emperor
 hallucinating on mescal
        in a hothouse San Diego
           before throwing TVs from the tenth floor.

They leave a devastated trail. From West
 to East they face the rising sun
like samurai saluting its red cone;
 warlords guarded by hoi polloi
        hardwired into what they do best,
           they keep on riding, knowing that they've won.

## STICKY FINGERS

Transitioning mega – don't need it now
the prescriptable band photo –
just the Warhol taut zipper slash
open on 1970
like a lysergic hologram

morphing from drenched colour into
cold diamonds, cocaine rocks,
street heroin. The sound on Sticky's hard
like gangsters taking someone out
undercover in a wet yard.

Stargroves, Olympic, Muscle Shoals,
you get Mick Taylor's seamless signature
a rainbow's curve of Chinese chords
so guitars-guerrilla on 'Sway'
he's like a blues academy.

A 1954 Fender Telecaster's
his slide-speak on 'You've Gotta Move'
done Mississippi-shop, white boy does black
as rootsy trans-cultural, and 'Bitch'
you get it hot as Thunderbird exhaust.

1970's bent red sunshine
optimal weird community: today
the window's irretrievably retro
the sunlight on it grainy – what hangs in
is coming – Dark Side of the Moon…

Sticky's romantic epic summary
of London's own grown up hard and defiantly
into US conquistadors, you hear
'Dead Flowers' – buy roses for your grave
and take it, all the living in between.

## FAREWELL TOUR 1971

Tequila sunrise. o.j.
grenadine and cactus liquor
backstage, burns in the viscera,

skews the tempo on 'Brown Sugar'.
They've outgrown the British circuit,
awkward with their past, the damage

done by hedonistic rampage.
Shambolic in the North, Richards
travels with his own Gestapo,

he's so out of time, the drummer
can't catch up until the end.
Something's changed. It's not Mick Taylor's

resourceful arpeggios,
it's a first move towards stadia
and impersonal rock aerobics.

'Midnight Rambler' gets a rethink,
'Wild Horses' turns a slow corner,
stripped and transparently poignant.

Leeds, Liverpool, Bristol, Glasgow,
their skunk-trail marks its territory
as slashed ammoniac solvents . . .

London's their extravaganza,
two nights under the Roundhouse rotunda,
out of sync except for Jagger's

furiously rotating bum
cupped in Mr Fish pink satin
encoring 'Street Fighting Man'. . .

## ABOUT FACE

Burroughs' *Naked Lunch* left on the stairs
at Cheyne Walk – a Panther paperback
bridging decades, junk on the map

as infiltrator to the cells,
the blue poppy as papaveracous
apotheosis

with silky hairs.
Two nights at the Lyceum as obit
to 1969 – a gypsy band

pulling in players like a tribe
real estated across the globe.
Nodded off, blanked out in the hall,

tented in ratty antique mink
Marianne overhears the deal –
30 million minus her,

a band offer from Atlantic
without the junky passenger.
Keith launchpads industrial fireworks at No 3,

orange auroral explosions that burn
intense fall out asymmetry.
He shuts in with his own coterie

the weirder than Rimbaudian weird,
psychonauts orbiting a star
sighted over Chelsea Harbour.

London's tea at the Dorchester
a Jaguar across Mayfair –
a nucleus imploding on itself,

crazy as Blake's Jerusalem,
its pop re-branded and the night
coming up like the Thames swallowed the sun.

## TROPICAL DISEASE

The drug's a muddy undertow –
smack in the Tropical Disease sessions,
insidious, 6000 pounds
per half kilo
delivered to Keith's Nellcôte pharmacy –

a Med locus, that shimmery
the sea cuts diamonds at the door.
The basement's hashed to foggy soup,
the stoned and a blood-sipping entourage
shattered across the cellar floor,

disjointed jams, disunity;
Jagger waiting like a tarantula
to inject poison in the song,
rushing his words like Slim Harpo
into a bluesy slurred scramble –

the meaning buried in the mix.
They're high and low
like hot and cold
no homeostasis in the blood.
The songs are dug out of malarial mud

rough, steamy and degenerate.
The 70s hang cryogenically
suspended, they're still 60s time,
apocalyptic flashbacks atomised
as residual fall out,

a band at thirty, exiled, burnt,
under continuous death threat
post-Altamont, displaced expatriates
ripping through its cultural gamut
in the near stultifying heat,

their dirty sound indicative
of a decade's tarnish, like grime
filmed on a black three tonnes Bentley,
their process a pre-punk up yours
indigenous notoriety –

Exile on Main Street chopped up raw
on squalid nights – the menu blues
and a crisp Chablis – ing a song
and go back to a seafood plate
to nibble at a lobster's claw.

## TROPICAL DISEASE A.K.A. EXILE ON MAIN STREET

Muddy as a river's shuffle with the tide, raw, squeezed and pulped, Exile is domestic blues, a Nellcôte basement one-off surge of tropical 1971: an excerpted time of

Stones

banditry: the displaced, druggy focus achieved by swipingly disruptive sessions built into a sound that's proto-punk by default, like it's the accidental demos for an album raffishly rehearsed and in part speculatively abandoned. Whatever year you catch it, it's incomplete, single-less, except for 'Tumbling Dice' and singularly rude. It's the lack of hooks as resources narrates the rushed impromptu songwriting, so that it's the texture compensates, a grainy blues jam with the colour separating from the sixties, like a strawberry Villefranche sunset bleeding into steamy storm whipped up by the mistral.

Tip

London sensibilities into a Monte Carlo casino milieu and they go subterranean and root right in the dark to record junk music that arguably dissolves the ambience of Scott Fitzgerald's dissolute Riviera novel *Tender Is the Night* into the Shirelles' Greatest Hits.

Marseilles

the ubiquitous heroin-gateway feeds Richards' dopamine receptor sites with top grade H – Thai heroin called cotton candy on account of its bright pink dusty sheen, like carbon emissions into the footprint, delivered by handgun-toting thugs in smart attaché cases into the inchoate resistantly unintelligible music. Exile can sound like one extended session, chopped into variants, or because of its lawless drive epic fuck-up, as non-linear as William Burroughs' *Naked Lunch* and as compulsively arresting.

One hundred degrees

down there; stripped off, insalubrious, a band underground trying to accelerate with bits into songs that don't gel, and was Mick Taylor's insidious intro to an increasingly destabilising habit – Corsicans in the cellar with half kilos of heroin priced at six thousand pounds cash – begun there in the airless, raunchy, ultimately despondent process?

Keith:

'If you're going to get into junk, it takes the place of everything. You don't need a chick, you don't need music, you don't need nothing. But it doesn't get you anywhere. It ain't called junk for nothing. Why did Burroughs kick it, after 25 years? He's thankful he kicked it, believe me. There's a lot of Chinese shit around. That's all I can say. That's another one of those rumours.'

Exile's

Seminal placing in Stones mythology defies the often sprawling mapping of its contents: it's Keith's Naked Lunch – an opiate gateway into rough trade rock metabolised through riffed equivalents of self-destruct that could have had the Stones ignominiously implode in a sticky, humid basement littered with bottles of Jack Daniels and Mafia-type dealers in top grade. It's the narcotic legend attached to Exile's making that precedes its skewed creative module, its essential blues churn never coming clean, rather like Richards' drug managed brain chemistry.

Exile's

a bootleggers' Stones-bank: all those roughs, demos, unvocalised instrumentals, jams, stops and starts liberated into unauthorised domain, and always for their illegality edgier than the commercially released product. What about trying I Gave You Diamonds You Gave Me Disease, the Exile on Main Street Outtakes as a Sister Morphine Production. 1 Exile on Main Street Blues 2 Got A Line On You 3 Good Time Women 4 Shake Your Hips 5 Hillside Blues 6 Sweet Virginia 7 Bent Green Needles 8 Loving Cup 9 Ventilator Blues 10 I Ain't Signifying 11 Let It loose 12 All Down The Line 13 Travelin' Man 14 Stop Breaking Down 15 Shine A Light 16 I'm Going Down

Overviewing

the traumatic dislocating experiencing of recording too much material with lack of disciplined focus, Mick Taylor commented: 'We suddenly found we had some new songs that were all good. I think *Exile on Main Street* is more forceful than *Sticky Fingers* but it's not as imaginative or adventurous. That's purely a personal opinion. No, there isn't any dissent within the band, surprisingly enough.'

An MT

critique is usually apologetically compromising; it evaluates the downside of the raucous, abandoned, mercenary material, the off-mike vocals fading in and out of the endemically dirty sound, like blue as a colour is shredded to swampy military camouflage – spinach greens and lemon and Sahara browns, as the guerrilla undertones. Richards' associative mood-board is more Reichstag grey and black in his recall of stomping the basement for unedited sound.

Keith

refocuses the environment as, 'like trying to record in Fuhrerbunker. It was that sort of feeling, very Germanic down there – swastikas on the staircase… Upstairs, it was fantastic, like Versailles. But down there it was Dante's *Inferno*.'

'Rocks Off'

'Rip This Joint' accelerate with almost hallucinated delirium in the bunker, with Jagger sounding like he's projecting tropical derangement to get it out of his nerves hot into sound. The oddness of this ragged new is its sexy subversive tangent: the tight, linear progression so central to characteristic smashes like 'Jumping Jack Flash', 'Honky Tonk Woman' and the driving hypnotic 'Brown Sugar' aren't integrated into Exile's decadently horny texture. Even the hit single 'Tumbling Dice' pulled from the album's essentially forgettable overlapping melodies lacks conviction and wobbles for lack of developing lyric, Jagger confessing to writing it casually, accidentally, while talking to the housekeeper about the high stakes gambling in the easily locatable casinos around the coast.

Cut Up

William Burroughs and Terry Southern materialised in the bunker like pharmaceutical holograms hoping to angle the band into writing a song for the soundtrack to the proposed movie of *Naked Lunch* that dipped off-radar, like an anti-gravity UFO sighting.

Exile's

the anti-hero narrative of Richards' descent into heroin addiction, and years of dysfunctional crashed chaos, as though the heavy initializing usage at Nellcôte provided him with a window on his own junk event-horizon, his literal whiteout. Disrupted by guitars going out of tune due to the humidity and by irregular uncoordinated and wasted sessions, and with Jimmy Price's and Bobby Keys' horns integral to the piratical sound, Exile has Richards as its druggy centrepiece, not

Jagger

who thought the sprawl 'lousy and lacking in concerted effort,' his distaste for shambolic squalor affecting the Slim Harpo-type vocals, in which the muffled phrasing is rushed and often inarticulate, as though waiting to quickly liberate himself from the dope-drenched basement into an alternative reality.

Desperate

measures ventilate. 'Your spine is cracking and your hands they shake/ when you're trapped and circled with no second chances/ your code of living is your gun in hand…' 'Ventilator Blues' with Mick Taylor's superlative guitar licks is quintessential desperado Exile: no way out because Richards has elected to drill for gold in his unventilated cellar, and in the process pull the manipulated Stones into a black hole.

It's a case

that Exile's titles are often more interesting than the throwaway lyrics that disappointingly undermine expectation. Nothing's worked on or crafted. The basic components remain basic, like black on black on black.

Inside Nellcôte

the cocktail of musicians, entourage, dealers and rogue drop-ins led to a fuzzy disdain for alert. Disliking the saturated drug ambience Charlie Watts and Bill Wyman were intermittent players unglued from the unstoppable boho partiers. While the occupants were watching television burglars made off in the migraine-inducing sunlight with nine of Richards' guitars, Wyman's bass and Bobby Keys' saxophone, 1972.

What do you

do?

Exile

marks a closure to the Stones as high-charting singles band, their depressed laconic figures and essentially unstructured writing entering their limbic groove as a predominant seventies characteristic, redeemed only by 1978's *Some Girls*, in which colourfully inflected hooks and variant poppy referents reinvented their sound as hit-makers with the number 1 disco influenced 'Miss You' that kicked up a storm across the planet, as reactivated frontline intelligence.

Exile's

garage; its colours like a blue light bulb in a black room or a black light bulb in a blue room. 'Sweet Virginia' and 'Torn and Frayed' profess Richards' ongoing preoccupation with country balladry, but again lack protein lyric, as though words were bleached by sunlight and the Stones; English sensibilities angular to mistral-dusted Mediterranean dazzle, after a lifetime experiencing diamond drizzled light from low grey London cloud ceilings.

Holing

up in the dark was to crunch London into basement dimensions, condense the capital into a cable-entangled, messy workspace, a pirate king's immersion into confused energies, as Exile's core: nothing to do for Richards but to listen to himself in an experimental garage,

listen to himself

do chemically adjusted music nailed as interloping licks pursuing that invisible chord again

like habituation to the blues

## VILLEFRANCHE

Clobbered with lobster pots, a fishing boat
trails out of harbour, a swishy mare's tail
of fuming bubbles throttled to a V,

the beaked prow bouncing as it slices chop.
A gypsified Keith Richards flops in shade,
the water-bed rolling like he's at sea,

glasses trained on a battleship's gun stacks,
anchored deep water in the grainy haze,
its crew drug-stashed with opium and hash . . .

He marks fleet-visitations in a book.
His parrot glowers like an orange firework
cascading into molten blue and green.

He's waiting for an E-type from Marseilles,
the Mafia dealer trafficking pure Thai
cotton candy – a pink-sheened heroin

he pays for with brick-sized bundles of notes.
It's gold dust to his cells, cool alchemy,
a chilly euphoric oblivion

like having a cold bulb on in the brain.
His dogs gorge pheasant on the balcony.
He's like an effete Baudelairean king,

the one whose blood is green syrupy ooze,
and who grows bored waiting for the next fix:
nothing entices, dogs, music or sex,

only anticipation of the cache
he'll grade by snorting through a rolled bank note,
then count the rest out like he's swatting flies.

## COCKSUCKER BLUES

The Robert Frank doc – shoot it hot
    on a customised DC-7
adaptive groupie same-sex sex
lubricated with a tequila hex
    entertains, popping the g-spot.

There's a ménage an entourage
    and cutie Truman Capote
so juiced and destabilised by rock
he spoons a cocktail cherry on his cock
    and collides with a stack backstage

too liquor-soaked to note the crash.
    In-flight fucking's Puerto Rican
D-cup babes, so stoned, elastic,
they're like pliant orgiastic
    moon-walkers giving head for cash.

It's glitzy drug-drenched 1972
    a degenerate apogee
for rock's royal family, they've got the taste,
dollars, eyeliner, rhinestone paste,
    a brattish ostentatious new.

The architecture's hits that smash
    America, pre-9/11
rat on its war economies
by gunning licks and travesties
    and giving sovereignty to trash.

The shooting rehabilitates
    transgressive states, they cross America
under surveillance, throw a TV out
10 floors to shatter in a parking lot
    and coolly burn out of the mansion's gates.

## LADIES AND GENTLEMEN

Quaaludes, a scarlet tequila sunrise,
    Seconal, Desoxyn, Keith flips
the Neiman-Marcus catalogue of dope
    at Hugh Hefner's heart-shaped Playboy Mansion
snakeskin boots wedged into a throw that rips
    a fault-line from a skewed nail-head.
*The Naked Lunch*: Terry wants raw hemp rope
    junk songs as Stones soundtrack, and bleeds
drawled sales chutzpah at a stoned Marshall Chess
    the project like a decommissioned jet
without a taker. The Stones sprawl excess
    as déclassé martian ambassadors
excluding all reality. Mick wears
    a purple rhinestone jumpsuit on/offstage
like reinventing gender and Keith's hands
    from shredding four nickel-wrapped steel guitar strings
at Chicago are sliced with ravaged cuts.
    A day framed into 1972
like looking out a plane window somewhere
    you'll never know, except it's physical,
a pool table with cubes of purple chalk,
    the underwater bar, someone turned blue
from a kilo of plant matter. A day's
    a life; the fear of being shot on stage
a constant: tequila and grenadine,
    kahlua and cream, ride on baby, ride,
to New Orleans, Alabama, the next stop
    extrapolating madness: they're so deep
the crowds are land mass, and Mick Jagger thumbs
    a paperback reprint of *The Big Sleep*.

## BYRON AND JAGGER

Byron's the sex addicted bitch
his serial conquests booting up his rage:
he swipes a wine-flecked lace cuff scorchingly

at Annabella's retroussé nose,
smashes a glass to littered brilliants
across the marble floor, pulls a corner

and rips the tablecloth into her lap.
His rage keeps gaining altitude;
its rumble stratospheric.

He needs a woman backways in.
The reverse like he makes a man –
matelot-vested gondoliers

back of green deadwater canals . . .
He's attitude fed alcohol.
He dreams of rocking in the Parthenon,

torching the place and up in hills
de-realising into myth.
Jagger's his flash-forwarded brain-child,

the frontman camping it to stadiums,
wealthier than a Saudi sheik
or plutocratic pharaoh,

deadlier than the Reichstag,
commissars, autocrats, dictators,
he controls youth with the sneer

of a knife cutting a lemon,
dances like a revivalist
steamily possessed in the Mississippi,

recruits the media Byron lacked
stomping his dead leg through a sitting room,
glowering with cyclic mania.

## THE BIG FREEZE (1972)

At Ocho Rios
Rastas toking ganja
cigars sedate Keith with burru

hypnotics played at his villa,
while the band at Terra Nova
pick at curried goat and akee,

like the menu's spicy voodoo.
Camaraderie's gone missing,
Keith's dysfunctionally bi-located,

face pinched like a death's head ring
grooved to an abraded finger.
He's defected as co-leader

of his nomadic
rock mercenaries. He's Napoleon;
his incommunication vatic:

the Caribbean turned to ice
each time he withdraws, a green jewel
signposted with cryptic lyrics.

Jagger's the *modus operandi*,
the *genius loci* of a studio
scored with bullet holes from cartels

scorch marks peppering the walls.
Business as usual is his role,
shaping miasmatic vocals.

Keith's principate of St Anne parish,
his stake of Jamaica's panorama's
like Napoleon's at Elba,

his exile deepening, like the sea
deleting tidemarks, jumbling up the coast
and repositioning what it sets free.

## GOAT'S HEAD SOUP

It's the dip off-radar: the displaced, rootless in exile nomadic album – Keith Richards stateless: the eviction suite, the Jamaican Rasta hangover, the neglected Stones resources post-Exile, as though they were attempting to re-harness their late sixties satanic aspects – Jagger as pouty, androgynous anti-hero Lucifer, stained by Meredith Hunter's blood in December 1969, the knife wounds inflicted

by

Hell's Angels, pooling into wound seepage big as the state of California, red as a dark red carnation. That chaotically lysergic quango on stage, studded biker jackets, biker boots, a Stones customised bodyguard whacking the hippified front rows with pool cues, thrusting their mud-crusted Harley choppers into the endemically stoned crowd with psychotic dissociation, a lawless maniacal assault on the druggy underbelly they smash as community.

Dancing with Mr D

re-invents the ritual kill, the rock shaman dealing death like Tarot cards, the singularly self-mythologized frontman projecting occult because he's blues turned into escalating dollars.

'Will it be poison put in my glass

Will it be slow or will it be fast? The bite of a snake, the sting of a spider A drink of belladonna in a Toussaint night Hiding in a corner in New York City Lookin' down a forty-four in West Virginia'

The gangsta-speak voodoo-inflected lyrics of 'Dr D' are Burroughs influenced as toxic subtext: the album version stripped of Mick Taylor's indomitably ripping solo that's the bootlegger's favourite: the link to 'Sympathy for the Devil' signature into the pungent Jamaican soup, most of the album recorded at Kingston's Dynamic

Sounds Studio, on account of Richards' criminal WANTED drugs legacy. Keith:

'Jamaica

was one of the few places that would let us all in. By that time about the only country that I was allowed to exist in was Switzerland, which was damn boring for me, at least for the first year, because I don't like to ski. Nine countries kicked me out, thank you very much, so it was a matter of how to keep the thing together...'

*Goat's Head Soup* is disintegrated content locked into Stones dirty grooves formula, heterogenous material , some of it like 'Silver Train' and 'Winter' recorded at Stargroves, London's Olympic Sound Studio in 1970, and revamped for GHS's indifferently mediated firepower.

Time-

slip back to 1973 and Jagger evaluates intense surges of bittiness at the core. 'Songwriting and playing is a mood. Like the last album we recorded [*Exile*] *Goat's Head Soup* was basically recorded in short concentrated periods. Two weeks here, two weeks there, then another two weeks. And similarly, all the writing was concentrated so you get the feel of one particular period of time. Three months later, it's all very different and we won't be writing the same kind of material again.'

GHS

is sonic home-lab toxicology, street drug poisons – there's a habit-lineage goes back to Thomas Chatterton's suicide on 24 August 1770 at Brook Street, Holborn, from arsenic poisoning, to Thomas De Quincey's inveterate opium habit, Gerard De Nerval's, Poe's, Baudelaire's, Harry Crosby's, Jean Cocteau's, Anna Kavan's, on the literary side, and in music, specifically blues, a dope/junk liberation epitomized by the South with Billy Holiday as its ruined centrepiece.

Obeah

voodoo: a goat's head boiling in a stewpot – the Stones cooking revenge as exiles kept integrated by Mick Taylor's eloquent guitar figures and glammed up by David Bailey for a photo-shoot for the album's mustard-yellow gatefold sleeve – the album's time-frame as Jagger emphasised specific, the last of the Stones' sixties overlap albums, with the druggy generation bleed of one decade into another.

'100

Years Ago' personifies tempo transition, a throwback rescued by urgent guitars, the retro window an emotional one – you can go back but only in memories trafficked from the basis of the present – 1973 in Stones' time, the same time you hear today listening to GHS in altered reality.

'Doo Doo Doo

Doo Doo (Heartbreaker)' rocks with street dirt desperation, a 10-year-old selling sex on the New York streets, typical Stones lawless controversy, break all the laws in life, break all convention in music, and do it guarded by lawyers who are rinsed in criminal motivation.

GHS

off the back of the Stones' celeb debauch 1972 US tour, much of it documented by Robert Frank's still commercially unreleased Cocksucker Blues, a slice of decadent slouch from the sybaritic camp is a curious mix of eclectic slung together bits, that like Exile is lean in melodic hooks, sustained writing time eroded by constant touring and immersion in a reality too idiosyncratically pampered to put reality up front. Launched into high life the Jagger/Richards ensemble began to lose street-cred on Goat's and to be insulated by fame and wealth. 'Coming

Down

Again' has a woman turning green from bad drugs, a slow melodic descent, but lacks real lyric engagement, like there's a die-off of rich lyricism that last got motivated, end of the sixties, 'Beggar's Banquet' and 'Let It Bleed' when touring was suspended and writing more sustainably focused, more rippingly in touch with the underbelly.

'Starfucker'

brokers punk – the track's energised into up-yours invective, the déclassé aristo yobbism the Stones adopt so well, Jagger's social aspirations, his deconstruction of class on his own terms as indomitable icon roughing up pretensions with hooligan vocals – the made-up petulant limp-wristed rocker throwing it back at NY celebs, the gay literati like Truman Capote, the lot, with a market trader's bawling oiky rudeness as closer to an album made in snatches, on the run, and because of its careless, reckless abandon, a worldwide No. 1 more on the momentum of unstoppable taboo status than merit: a cops and robbers, mafia and CIA, cartel and drug mule harassed Richards.

1973

J. G. Ballard's *Crash*, as the erotics of car ergonomics in collision with bodies, William Burroughs' *Exterminator*, as drugs lab ET, Richard Brautigan's *The Pill Versus the Springhill Mine Disaster*, for quirky weird and B. S. Johnson's singularly British experimentation *Aren't You Rather Young To Be Writing Your Memoirs?]*

12/13 November

cutting his wrists in the warm bath, leaving half a bottle of brandy beside the bath with a note attached, 'you'll need this when you find me.'

# PART 4

# MEMORABILIA/BONUS MATERIAL

## BUYING STONES BOOTLEGS AT THE STABLES

A reconstructed yard, a Camden squeeze,
snuck back of a smudgy sage-green canal,
it's punchy in the cold, breath atomized
into blue hexagonal puffs –
vaporized carbon dioxide diamonds
signposting dispersed energies. I pick

my way in segues through the compressed crush,
Spanish, French, platinum Slovakians
freezing the moment with phone-cameras
into a digital shoplift. The rush
keeps peaking: back of the Thai noodle stalls
I find my dealer and I want the lot

69–78 outtakes, live,
raw garage at Olympic – hooty sounds
riffed by a blues Al Queda with a look
that's generic defiant attitude,
biro-barrel skinny, punk Londoners
skinning convention alive like a mule,

smashing their carbon footprint on the globe.
The market accelerates to a jam,
slow motion foot traffic full on by 3,
there's Amy Winehouse in ripped skinny jeans
looking like she's been up a century
and arrived tomorrow or yesterday

in a personal space-time. I talk up wants
as needs: a 68 Chelsea rehearsal,
a casual slouch through river-muddy blues
at Cheyne Walk with hazy puffs of mist
throwing striptease figures over the bridge.
We share green tea in a blue paper cup

branded Caffe Nero: the day breaks up
in busy schedule: I go off with sounds
lifted from other times for completion,
go sit back to a wall by the canal's
oozy steps – and a tug churns into view
frothing white water and called Baby Blue.

## HAM YARD W1

Time-cut 2010: Six months of Wednesday 9.30 a.m. hyper-energised photo-shoots like slicing time into visual frames, me working exhibitionistically across the derelict piss-drenched 0.75 acre Soho yard for Gregory Hesse's Canon angles; the light sharp like cutting your finger on a tin, or drizzled like steamy urban puff. Greg's technology comprised a Canon Ultrasonic 28-200mm, loaded with black-and-white Ilford HP5 film, 36 exposures available each explosively angularly choreographed shoot, an unrepeatedly impacted interactive 15 minutes that left both of us emotionally used up from the intense hit and run dynamic.

Our work incentive as Mod aficionados was using me as the focus to make a visual document of a cratered yard that housed Ronan O'Rahilly's legendary Scene club, as the epicentre of Mod culture in the early 1960s, was accelerated by the news that the hotel chain Firmdale, owned by Tim and Kit Kemp, had exchanged contracts to buy Ham Yard for around £30m to build a luxury 100-room hotel, plus 50,000 square feet of housing on an indigenously proto-hipster landmark. To the coolly dressed two-tone tonic-mohair suited Faces or individualists in pilled-up 1964, the site was also known as pill yard, due to the gravitation of speed dealers there, selling Drinamyl pills shaped like purple Viagra diamonds both in the yard and inside the 200 capacity Scene club, a blacked out unlicensed basement on what was a bomb-site back of the Lyric Tavern on Great Windmill Street.

You can't recreate history; it's a series of inaccessible space-times hijacked by imagination, but essentially wiped, like watching the empty grey sky fill in with its floaty cloud architecture after a plane's departed, so Greg and I optimalised the acute present with its zillions of localised photons, dodging the XXL waist black sacks for shots fired like a gun with the silencer on.

Ham Yard which owes its name to a lowlife pub called the Ham in existence there in 1739, and used by robbers and stick-up highwaymen has a defiant counterculture history rooted in music. During the 1920s' fizzy jazz milieu it was home to the Ham Bone Club for liberated, short-skirted partiers soaking up gin and sexually charged blues, while in the 1950s the cellar pioneered Cy Laurie's Skiffle Club, soon to be Cy Laurie's Jazz Basement, and a dancing academy during the day, before becoming the seminally cutting-edge druggy Scene club in the 1960s. It was there the likes of the Rolling Stones, the Who, the Pretty Things, the Action and the Animals tore down the walls with their sweaty anarchic volume-up, maximum R&B rip the joint dynamic.

Something of the intensely personalised projection of my poetry performances with the Ginger Light permeated compressed 15mins sessions in which spontaneously thrown shapes motivated the accidental immediacy of Greg's shots. We converted the commercialized yard into a performance space invaded by offloading vans, truck-reversals, quizzical property surveyors, territorial employees of adjoining office space, none of who succeeded in breaking into our defensively charged time-zone.

The human body is limited by a number of instinctual variant poses, and working within our individual capacities we attempted to intensify rather than diversify a particular look, linking my contorted posture and expressively thrown up arms to the abraded surface of a black peeling wall, a mesh fence post, or simply the menacing atmospherics of a place islanded into residual decay, all DNA traces of customised first-wave Mods rubbed into the yard's gritty dirt.

Time-Cut, the Scene, July 1964: The Jagger phenomenon: 135 lbs of skinny dance compression on a compacted 10 ft stage, the unlived-in black Anello & Davide Chelsea boots click abrasively like castanets, the singer's provocative striptease steps, one foot crossed mincingly over the other in a flurry of yellow nose coned maracas is so delinquent camp, it's both contagiously arrogant and punkishly sexualized travesty. He's squeezing raw R&B juice out of the Stones' first full-on unstoppable chart smash, a vandalised speeded-up cover of 'Not Fade Away' that explodes into manic garage, the equivalent of a Ferrari's acceleration from 0–60mph in 3.5 seconds.

He's the look Mods can't fix or dare emulate without being a copyist, the sexual ambivalence restructuring the black wool Cecil Gee blazer, three-buttons, waisted, slim lapels, worn insolently over a Polo-mint white fly-fronted tab-collar shirt, the figure forming low-rise silver wool hipsters from John Stephen's His Clothes theming cool with dressy elegance. And for all the intransigent streetwise attitude he projects, the sensibility is one of intelligent remove from the crowd's increasingly liberated hysteria each time he surges into the untutored footwork he's learnt impromptu from projecting on condensed stages. Jagger's so effortlessly the look he's creating it so as to be it, hair worn long over the collar and in girlie bangs at the front, that Mods won't incorporate him into their aesthetic, because to them his look's too accessorized, too individualized a fashion moment. The black painted walls sweat and walk in on the crowd as he squeezes the harmonica to a Jack the Ripper alley wail on 'Confessin' The Blues', his dance steps choreographing the song's dejected mood-board.

The remaining band member's meshed into the flat visceral sound are bleached into off-message insignificance by Jagger's upfront confrontational energies, his physicalized focus of the song becoming its sonic figure, so he's its mobility, and the front row dive at his elusive shape-shifting ankles, trying to grab something of him, before a bulky gofer's savvy crunches the offenders back into line.

You can't both be him and watch him perform, his vulnerability being sited in his essential passivity – the musical offensive screens his physical fragility, his size-zero androgyny is minded, despite the band's kamikaze rip each time they come on in a policed precinct to tear it up with insurgent bad boy blues lifted from black.

Jagger's Scene club reinventions are like Dilly rent around the corner – a transgressive fact you fixate on to lose, because he's so far ahead of gender preconceptions, he's always going to win. When he's gone, the floor's littered with pills, cans, and the fretwork graffiti nailed by his Cuban heels. A girl's crying by the exit, another's slashed her number in red lipstick on the wall. It's over, 30 imperiously burn-out tribal Stones minutes – the Jagger phenomenon – the Mississippi Delta impersonator in clothes you'd die for. Outside it rains; the yard rinsed by the percussive shower that drenches fans running all the way to the tube at Piccadilly Circus to go under in 1964: a busy slice of time programmed into two- minute pop songs – 'Not Fade Away' (Petty/Hardin), and accelerating towards the end of time in the cosmic microwave background radiation.

Time Cut 2010: After the shoot Greg and I go talk and review a printed wallet of black-and-white photos from the previous week at Bar Bruno, an unpretentious, hyperactive native Soho café on the junction of Peter Street and Wardour Street and chill over mint tea in the conversationally loud greasy-spoon ambience. I tell Greg how I find myself often squatting down, compelled to make contact with the yard's fissured asphalt surface, as though looking for signs to the place written into its compacted urban dirt, like micro-fault lines. There's a cyan arrow and serial demonstrably painted there as part of the Thames blue ribbon network.

On one occasion I bought a bunch of dark red M&S roses to the shoot, as a prop, and we called it the Ham Yard funeral session; and left the roses bang up against a boarded window of the black flaking façade that was the Scene as a gesture of improvised street glamour. Each shoot was an affirmative last stand, a retrieval of a soon to be submerged space by two thin interactive figures ritualizing place: nowhere to run and 500 exposures bringing it all defiantly home.

## TONGUE AND LIP

A lipstick-red sensuous scrolled logo
iconic anarchic fat wagging tongue
(John Pasche commissioned 1969)
like liberated big mouth oral sex
a hot licks avenging fellatio
the Jagger bigger than a sunflower pout
raw streaming valorised energies
the preening snappy bitchy crunch that's phrased
so insolently it's oligarch-rock
with infectious camp twist, the blues wrung out
like faded jeans, bleached indigo.
That gobsmacking scarlet Kali-inspired
protruding splash initialized on Sticky Fingers
it authorizes lawless attitude,
a tribal posse, done for £50
a £200 bonus in 1972
for its global attention-grab, cool rule
over accelerated community,
no font on playful banditry, a frontline slash
branding firepower like rocket exhaust.

## POP SLICE

A fuzzy time-slip: Joe Meek's bathroom studio
improvised hands-on compressed circuitry
pop firsts – he out-indies indie
accidentally: pre-Beatles, pre-Stones
lippy-red E-type pill-head entrepreneur
same-sex-attracted fucked-up autocrat.
You get the beat merchants, Mersey Doo-wop
Teddy boy rock blues copyists synergised
into flat boxy sound and R&B
squeezed from a raucous wailing harmonica
like blues exhaust: accelerate 'Come On'
it's quantum leap's to number one, a spook
hiking Stones hoodlum into the lower charts
'Come On' initializing tribal brawl rock licks
as up yours. All those transient pop hooks
that got sucked into a black hole
they're one-offs bleached into disinformation.
'Come On' was sticky impersonation
and rude on Decca.
                    Go out into the Soho rain
those days – you get the industry's colour
like low-cloud ceiling: and Pat Valerie's
bohemian revenge, five gritty Stones in there,
moody, dejected, filtering sugars
into the steamy English breakfast tea.

## COPS AND ROBBERS

Alice Diamond, Queen of the Forty Thieves.
minky, vampish, pouty, expensive shoplifters
nicking Debenhams furs, Selfridges accessories,
dark red smoochy Guerlain bullets,
paste and diamond popped into pointy bras
offloading to boosters in spivvish cars
designer stock – they beat men black and blue
hoodlum dikes and not gangster's molls
(a subject for the Rolling Stones)
Alice Diamond butch diva with a gun,
serial kleptomaniac driven by the rush
for chilly sparklers, lining up cocaine
like accelerated stardust circa 1923
(a subject for the Rolling Stones)
before the firm, Nash gang and Richardsons'
cool-suited boxy swagger, slablike thugs
in paisley ties, the streets were Alice's
for lawless grabs.
                       This geezer lubes the threat,
it's Reggie, or it's Ronnie, racketeers
who'll do arson or deconstruct your knees
while wearing Dior scent. Alice goes stomp
like a feisty rocker, stomp, stomp, stomp,
(a subject for the Rolling Stones)
kicks off her boots, fans out her red-nailed toes
and fizzes tonic into sniffy gin.

## MICK JAGGER'S LIPSTICKS 1972–1978

Neon-red         lippy pout like eroticised tantra
Persian red      the matte simmer of a hooker's fellatio
China red        oriental curve of elastic constraint
Scarlet          hot gloss mouthing a phrase like snake-bite
Red-violet       popping a violet crème on the tongue

Ruby             waiting for romance on the Siberian Express
Carnelian        smoking dope in a pink marble bath
Crimson          a mood that sits on a red cushion
Vermilion        hormonal tempo with vicious texture
Strawberry       a love-heart explosive with blues dollars

Indian red       the bindi colour of a brothel's walls
Rose madder      soft tone degrading like a peeling rose
Sangria          the taste of edible red vowels
Alizarin         a sneer framing forty thieves with red eyes
Russian red      a full-on Moscow sunrise seen through a diamond

Carmine          interzone between diva and pasha
Burgundy         brutal cupidity sipping fame
Tomato red       the shimmy importuning focus
Maroon           vintage car paint given rehab style
Blood red        vampirical lick at the moment's sugar coating

PERFORMANCE

Powis Square blocked into Portobello
    community, Gandolf's Garden
its avatar, acid ubiquity
    there, as an orange Notting Hill rainbow
1968, the Cammell shoot drug-dipped

in queer hood meets ambiguous pop star
    Chas as the vicious drug-psycho
hammering Joey, it's gang extortion
    the sort done at the Blind Beggar
as killing for company, a handgun

as PR, it's the post-Krays milieu,
    the camp chalk-stripes lubed up on gin
and speed. Turner's psychedelics are soft
    confection, a liquorice-all-sorts chew
with psychoactive levity, he sees

reality as a 3-D aquarium
    of hallucinated thought-waves, the girls
do any shade of sex and same-sex too
    like massaging a crimson plum,
and Turner's sybaritic gigolo

to every sensual flavour, twists it so
    he decodes Chas, hijacks the gangster's mind
like burning a cloned car on the Westway,
    snorts Chas's psyche, like it's blow;
they come together like they're acting gay.

The sixties die in a Notting Hill Square
    as a hedonistic memo, a grab
at everything, a decade that's so fast
    it never happened, they were standing there,
right in the present and it's called the past.

# PART 5

# THE RONNIE WOOD YEARS: 1975–

# THE ROLLING STONES

Sainted by notoriety
they're photographed by a bulldozered site,
cables exposed to bypass overhaul,

the hotel backgrounded as a glass cliff.
They're King crows parading in leopardskin
and cavalierly biffed knee-boots.

They wear their legend in deep-grooved skin tracks,
as though a creature roughed a hide
in crocodilian epidermis.

It's like they've died and been reborn again,
played tricks with time to always be the same
persons trapped by a hedonistic warp.

They're liver indestructible,
four decades of rocky empties glitter
behind them as a slaughtered galaxy.

They've burnt up continents in a cortège
of funeral limos. Thunder in the air.
The town silent, like it awaited sacrifice.

Guitar power's only half of it:
the singer's rush drives a trajectory
that hangs the moment between blues and death,

the skimming bird dipping the waterfall
shattering white force in a pool.
They've written rock riffs into history

and never stood back from those energies.
They're scorched by chords; their artistry's
enduring as pharaonic dynasties.

They stand exposed to hard Miami light,
dark glasses keeping the intruder out
and wait to gun high voltage at the night.

## A DIFFERENCE OF CIGARETTE ANGLES (KEITH AND RONNIE)

Richards and Woods –
dark mess of rucked up, slept-in crow-black hair,
an unkempt, dishevelled architecture,
spiky, Red Indian lacquered mops,
are paradigms of angled fags –
resistant cigarette stylists…
With Richards the filter's wedged dead centre
like a fixed point of gravity,
the blue spiralling curl of Marlboro smoke
looping back to the nostrils, leathering
the pigment, like the parched terrain
of the red Nevada desert.
Sometimes on stage the cig cooks left corner,
the angle sluttishly accidental,
the campish, defiant affectation,
part nicotine-need, part image.
Wood's is more basic, pedestrian,
as though his lungs have converted to smoke –
inhalation and renounced oxygen
as fuel for living. Ronnie's bonhomie
sanctifies smoking like a Ferrari needs juice,
as a component of chemistry.
His position's right and left of centre
like the parameters of his playing,
a smoker eating up three packs a day,
utilitarian habit.
Richards is cooler – he projects disdain,
the cigarette as need and image accessory,
the hit sanctifying charred lungs
the colour of a chestnut mare.
60 a day, fired-up on nicotine,

his fretwork's concentrated, and his riffs
spectacularly retro: punched-in fag skewed,
like the song off-centre, drooping ash
flickering orange, as legs splayed open,
he plugs the power into 'Jumpin' Jack Flash'.

## STONES GENE

A chromosomal sensibility-type,
a Stones gene, rogue adaptogen, RS
initialized in a pasta-twirl double helix
written into futures, their type travels
like scratched memories of 3,000 coloured lights

fixtured like a Las Vegas casino
into hallucinated dazzle, 1975
real time, if it existed, history's
a series of pop moments randomised
as killer hooks we anthologise

as optimal adrenalin bullets.
A flatbed truck trawls down Fifth Avenue
1 May 1975, the rocky belt
'Brown Sugar' crunched rudely from a wooden plank
as a crowd-stopping scorcher, a pop brawl

like facing down an irate street-trader.
Mick's silk pyjamas, were they fuchsia pink
or turquoise on stage? Someone remembers
the detail coded in a neural link
as extravagant retrieval, hot pink

like glazed coating on a sugared almond.
That funeral haul of stretch limos across the States,
dope-smoke mushrooming out of smoked windows,
state troopers snouting then at gunpoint out
for possession under a blank Arkansas sky.

The gene's resistant, jumps generations,
but pops up as phenotype, a lawless quirk
of reconstructed creativity
that's attitude, a reckless aesthetic
like living faster than the speed of light.

## SEVENTIES

A slab of exhausted orange sunlight
   activates urban reported sightings
on burn-out: what's it in the LSD
   does dystopian psychedelics
Ballard's collisional fetishised *Crash*
   the Stones laconic *Goat's Head Soup*
off-thrust directives: 'Coming Down Again'
   its centrepiece, like a blue traffic-light
as altered state: the band deplete focus
   by mega-touring – Crowley's lawlessness
inflected into travestied makeup
   boho sexualized entourage
an empire migrating across the globe
   riffing a scarlet boulevard
with 'Midnight Rambler' – it's the studded whip
   lashed on the stage as frontline threat
throws shapes for real – a decade in and out
   of criminal scandal the Stones
are déclassé bandits decorated in paste.
   The seventies implode with sixties
overload; Burroughs at Duke Street St James'
   fucks with the order – scientology
his transient mapping through drink and drugs
   and picking up rent at Piccadilly,
Dr Benway, a smart-suited alien
   slashing into The Wild Boys, Nova Express,
morphing weird into the accelerated capital
   that brought him down pre-garage punk
yob three-chords subversive supremacy.
   The Stones sound Stones 'Dancing with Mr D'
the ethos altered, but its momentum
   left running like a limo to explode

in crumpled flame. Teens rip up rock format
    Rotten vs Maggie's handbag,
a deconstructive gobbing anarchy
    with Ballard's *High-Rise* winning into place.
A fast and edgy dirty kick-ass sneer
    boots up *Some Girls*, resistant, opportune
chart rehab scorcher to the flattened times
    that come down like smashing a site
for serial repurposing on Canary Wharf
    another tower for a plane to point through.

## SOME GIRLS

Boulogne–Billancourt, five miles west of central Paris, Pathe Marconi Studios sited back of Renault HQ, weird psychogeography there for a time-slip regeneratively combative collision with punk: the Stones look still unapologetically sixties in 1977, contestable then, but now an unalterable signature, like casual disdain, and London – untutored anti-pop kamikazes – the Pistols its virulent spearhead of graffiti scratching chords

*like*

tagging Belsen in vermilion noodles on a Wembley yard. RS in directionless free fall minus Mick Taylor's eloquently descriptive mood-board licks

### KR

'It hit us by surprise. But he left us in the lurch. Suddenly you're looking for the second violin somewhere. He was an incredible player, but when he left us and you got to do those things yourself, it gets interesting.'

### Girls

refocuses the Stones into real time, rather than redundant exoplanetary celebs occupying substances-reality in rootless drift, attempting somehow to reconstruct their past achievements with unfocused depleted energies.

### From the off

*Girls* burns grittier and jumps red lights: tiny control room like a pilot's cockpit, a 60s' desk from Abbey Road – again a confused dissolve of decades in one-time, Stones time. You can't retrieve the past, but its molecular drizzle is always in your neurons, and how to connect with the present like saturated colour, so you displace the sometimes obstructively intrusive past.

### 'Miss You'

does that, configuratively reinvents. A Studio 54 disco beat with crunching unnerving guitars instead of predictable Philadelphia-style strings – instantly hooky and transitional and sparkly as space junk to a moon-tracker, you get James 'Sugar Blue' Whiting, found busking in the Paris Metro hijacked into colouring a harmonica solo like biting into a miked Granny Smith, with its crisp distressed messaging adding subway rough to exuberant disco passages. It's a typical Stones infection of a predictive genre disarranged for 1977 – take the clean out and do guitar dirt over beats and rhythms.

### Back

of 'Miss You,' not in it, 'Disco Inferno' by The Trammps, George McCrae's 'Rock You Baby,' The O'Jays…

### Girls

sees the Stones accelerating rather than floating into scorching business, 'When the Whip Comes Down' is ratty as punk, with adept musicianship – the street theme of selling sex incorporated into the bullet speed.

### KR

'The punks had the energy and attitude and presentation more than the actual music. I went to places like CBGB's, but I was in and out. But the punk thing had been coming over from England, and Mick always had a keen ear for anything new. I think it caught his attention, and so we transported it to Paris. *Some Girls* is a review of where Mick was going out to – one minute, slumming it down at CBGB's, the next going uptown to Studio 54.'

And irreverence:

'black girls just want to get fucked all night' – do they? But in Jagger's contemptuous index of experience, you don't doubt his do, as emotional accelerants to unlimited sexual availability in a neronic débâcle where groupies and Studio 54 highballing fashionistas merge like two sex corporates. New York disco bled into intransigent punk. The Stones had rebellious sophistication, London punks glue, speed, poverty and explosive acrimony and a complete deficit of decadent sensory experience programmed experientially into the Stones, who iconoclastically helped break down preconceived class barriers and re-emerge as déclassé aristos in the pop autocracy. Jagger's libidinous repertoire or menu of multinational flesh sounds gourmandised and likely to incite American feminist warriors.

## Drinks

for guitars. Jack Daniel's, Jim Beam, George Dickel, Cutty Sark, Benjamin Prichards, Knob Creek, Four Roses, Glenmorangie, J&B, Isle of Jura, Mull, Skye, grainy, malty, seaweedy, liver-altering poisons.

## There's blue rarified air

Appalachian space too 'Imagination' and 'Far Away Eyes' in which spatialized balladry, vocally and instrumentally dyed blue, (cyan, peacock, ultramarine), and Keith's Canadian heroin warrantry personalisation 'Before They Make Me Run,' leave off consolidated punk offensive for tightly self-reflective songs in which reactive personal loss is filtered into slower tempo climacteric pop of a kind that counteracts assault, while remaining hieratically taut.

## 'Respectable'

hits in as focused punk-rock, disarming first-wave anti-pop noise investors by its rude scare me up delivery, picking up on energies already programmed into the Stones and viciously redirecting them into typical mean aggro misogyny.

The one cover

here, a rough-edged revamp of The Temptations' 'Just My Imagination Running Away With Me' provides some insolent tough with muddy guitars and Jagger's pimpish overtones – he's still the indomitable trickster strutting it on top of the world exuberantly in black PVC jeans and cerise Converse All Star to outpunk punk like a cherry on a marron glacé.

'Shattered'

is a brainstorming narration of an economically downturned New York, 'go ahead bite the Big Apple / don't mind the maggots' that brings endgaming into demented acceleration. 'Love and hope and sex and dreams / are still surviving on the streets': it's the focus that disperses punk into an often inchoate saliva tsunami, and has the Stones revved to imploding in the course of flightpath delivery.

Farrah

Fawcett, Lucie Ball, Raquel Welch, Judy Garland and Marilyn Monroe get trashily de-poshed on a citric-blocked Peter Corriston cover, each of the Stones dragged up with a shocking red lipstick slash, as part of the re-emergent confused gender times liberated by punk's look – a deconstruction of Mod into urban guerrilla- disarranged chemically sprayed hair, plastic jeans, sloganed Japanese influenced design T-shirts, bondage, travestied tartan, leopard-print coats, spiderweb mohair, distressed muslin shirts, greaser jackets, slim leather ties

and the Stones

lifted bits into their looks anthology, as archetypal stylists, expensively dandifying deconstruct with their signature look, synonymous with debauched bohemians degrading classical lines into pop culture, 1978, *Some Girls*.

## DISREPUTABLE

    Resistant generic seditionaries
        Stones VS punks – teen bad boys on the block
    'White Riot' offensive, kill yr idols
        insurgent London three-chorders
    doing a Jack the Ripper on the groomed
        rock plutocrats: Johnny Rotten
    'the Stones should have retired in 1965'
        the fatwahed invective like carjacked paint
    a nick on a black Bentley's cellulose
        accessorised for customised fetish.
    New Wave antipathy to old totems
        the Iron Cross rebranded, can your hair
    a chemical tomato red, street-roughed
        like Hitler's college-boy-cut done spiky.
    Camden attitude doesn't compromise
        disreputable DNA
    the *Some Girls* mojo, a new shattering
        of rejuvenated juiced energies
    out-punking punk's offensive – and the look
        don't go there, for dandified slouch,
    you'll never copy Stones cool, it's real deal
        aristo-casual, red velvet flat cap
    on the frontman's helium levity
        a smart vampirical androgyny:
    and Keef's guitar weaponry, newly sourced
        MXR effects pedals, phaser
    and analogue delay. The frontline's war,
        'Respectable' 'When The Whip Comes down,'
    re-energised grooves, both boots in the face
        effrontery, coming back again
    on top: they plug in and it's hotter live
        facing down the times – do or die –
    storming the present's the way to survive.

# LONGEVITY

To some, the Stones were a sort of unkillable, thuggish, cultural voodoo, who continued, as degenerate bohemians, to periodically stick sharp dirty pins into the mainstream. To others they were a dedicated kamikaze institution, who would one day collectively implode on stage into physical death. But for now they were an irrepressible phenomenon, with Jagger's ineffably energised camp, all ten stone of his goji-juiced homeostatic reserve, launched like a hyperactive flamenco dancer, against the strutting thrust and counterthrust of the buccaneering guitarists, Keith Richards and Ronnie Wood. It was principally Jagger's continued act of flouncing, typically provocative misogyny, mixed with an undeniable plutocratic savvy, that kept the Stones sashaying their imperious way across the planet, leaving unimaginable carbon footprints, as their residue of brand excess.

## JACK & GINGER

Jack Daniel's spiced with whooshy dry ginger
no tidal mark to the river's
brain and liver assault
the ginger's the trickster comedian
in *Dirty Work* – a toxic signature
go 10 or 12 unmeasured liberal dollops
and they're red thunder to guitars
'Knock Yer Teeth Out' 'Had It With You'
like a petrol bomb message
in a lit bottle.
The aggressive rough demos source anger
like a blast shuttle's 750 tonnes
of liquid helium
only it's rock with a blues torque
and the ones you never hear
'Baby What You Want Me To Do' (Jimmy Reed)
Otis Redding's 'I've Got Dreams
To Remember' (he reviews them from death)
and the drummer's disruptive air-pocket
needs levelling with heroin
to ZERO that's an O
like vertigo or a snowflake
falling on a peak in Acapulco.

## MISMANAGED STRIPTEASE

The bunker book: *Cities of the Red Night*
Burroughs' viral creep, tropical pandemic,
how do you shoot a rose without destroying it,
reintegrate its dark red dispersal?
*Dirty Work* comes up period, Pathe Marconi,
mashed up personalities, 1985,
snappy as a zesty seafood plate's tang
and toxic. Charlie's dipped on heroin
and band dissolution: he takes the lift
and drops 100 years, forward or back
and emerges a white-haired Chinaman.
The studio's fight, separationist bleed,
Keith's Biff Hitler Trio versus Jagger,
fractured howling jamming that won't shut down
like a car horn blocked in an underpass.
Work happens independently, like planes
network the globe without our tracking flight,
just hearing drone. 'One Hit (To The Body)'
slams things like a messy in-cabin flight.
'Gonna pulp you to a mass of bruises
'cause that's what you're lookin' for';
the episodic smash doing the trick
take no prisoners unless you're a cannibal.'

## INDESTRUCTIBLE

Resistant immune-deficiency
like bluesmen do
stakeholders in shattered longevity
you map Keith Richards' epidermal faults
the wear's like track on London underground
the crunching ozone-whiffy Central Line's
scarlet attack, and Jagger's too
impacted facial zoning's grooved with tours
like g-forces at re-entry
8 times faster than a bullet.
                              1978–2013
you see degenerate process, a band
delivering liver damage:
Burroughs maintained cell-alteration from junk
inhibits cancer, and he could
metabolize diamonds to reshape shape.
Collective Stones prescribed and unprescribed
would make a pharmaceutical anthology
of scripted poetry.
                    The sound defies
biology, like compressed aviation –
fighter-jet exhaust fed through the speakers
and for the drummer in tour-intervals
                        a window on serenity

Yellow Square – Prithhivi  (matter or earth)
Silver Crescent – A pas  (water)
Red Triangle – Agni or Tejas  (fire)
Blue Circle – Vayu  (air)

you visualize these, each as a dissolve
into a clear window: the Stones track on
as rock licks circus: monitored heart-rates
indestructibly factored into time
like thunder crashing through the atmosphere.

## VOODOO HOODOO

It's all tangential, the extended jams,
the centre somewhere, like a bee's radar
piloting a honey jar,
'Blinded by Rainbows', speedy dirty grooves,
African licks, reinventing Exile,
the rum, Sambuka, Guinness rhythm reservoir,
the endemic Mick/Keith antipathy
exchanging notes about a soccer match
before splitting to separate corners
as indomitably conflicting avatars
propelled together at the ravaged core
of crunching rockers, 'Sparks Will Fly': rehearsals shatter
in a spacy Toronto aircraft hangar,
the album so locked into underground,
the sound's a skinny T-shirt undersized,
a Jaguar revving in a bank vault,
a kick ass mamba execration
like skinning python in the kitchen..
'String us up and we still won't die' Keith warns,
as accusatory blade-pointing dare.
Voodoo's alliterative – volatile, vexed,
vivacious, vociferous, venomous,
all the vs, and explosively hot live,
return to tough, Kurt Cobain's suicide gunned away
by a demonstrative cobra attack.

## 40 LICKS (BACKSTAGE)

The E-Trade online stock-broker patron's
    400 million gross does right
like helium mining on a mini-moon.
    They're four skinnies in black first night
at Boston, nervous like weak gravity

kicked balance backstage, like rock astronauts
    adjusting to the ISS,
loud primal drums tribal on the PA,
    lipstick traces caking a glass,
the licks they're revamping out of the vaults

like popping frozen bodies from Alcor
    into time-slipped immediacy.
The wait's like pre-second big bang, the stitch
    on a red button looping free
as irritant detail, and the last ditch

anxiety the hair dye's missed some grey
    as informing on real-time age
the air-cabin pressure to defy time
    deployed as physicals on stage
like rumbled thunder. It's part disbelief

you're really seeing them, compels, but now,
    they write smoke-signals with a joint,
a contrailed S, a vaporizing B,
    and Charlie tools an off-blue collar point
into exact placement, a jittery

shattering soaked up from the other side
    and at a nod Keith charges through
the curtain, guitar levelled like a gun,
    open-tuning directing it
the scorching uptake to 'Street Fighting Man'.

## A BIGGER BANG

The river's unstoppable flow
a guitar-driven
green-skinned Nile or Congo,
the riffs on it co-extensive with time,
the Stones on the road
like reading global blood-pressure
an ECG read-out
of catastrophic apocalypse
the road that only goes one way
to accelerated liquidation,
burning towers, corporate giants
evacuating cities in their jeeps
under a dragon-shaped smoke cloud
chasing their shoulder.
The band's the epic
soundtrack
amped-up anaesthetic
for final things — the President
crashing into his swimming pool
torched by a bomber in his suite,
his suit finned by red flames.
The road churns on —
their thunder roofing stadiums
1.5 million an hour
dollar bravura
virtuoso circuitry —
a Jagger, Richards, Wood, Watts, turbo-thrust
at making out with history
in buckskin boots and edgy coats —
a plutocratic rock circus
working the edge — it still goes on,
power as it's driven right to the stage hem
like an electrocuting hurricane.

## TWICKENHAM

The incongruously age-decayed Rolling Stones performed at Twickenham Stadium on their *Bigger Bang* global tour, parading their cryogenic longevity, and charting the band's phenomenally resistant durability.

If the Stones in the 21st century appeared morphed into a post-biological vacuum, in which teeny 28" waists defied a ravaged biography of recklessly lived-in facial wrinkles, then they endured as generic stadium dinosaurs, still plugging their contagious sixties' hits into the bankable present.

One of their two nights at Twickenham, as part of the band's riotously hedonistic eighteen-month sojourn across the planet, on the *Bigger Bang* tour that had grossed over £200m, in a blitzkrieg of adrenalin, popped endorphins and broken strings, a vast, timeless, pyrotechnical ritual, presided over by Richards' three-chord guitar surges, and the dervish theatricals of Jagger's hip-shimmying, shoulder-shaking, finger-pointing strut, bitchy as drag, and apparently physically unstoppable.

Watching the stage that night, appropriately saturated in red light, as Jagger, in a red trilby and red velveteen coat, spat out an epic, vehement 'Sympathy For the Devil', matched by Richards' incendiary signature guitar solo, and a vermilion supernova of accompanying fireworks, it was clear that a Stones concert is unquestionably at the centre of the known universe.

REVIEW

Their skinny majesties, the Rolling Stones, last night played a Philadelphia gig, on their *Bigger Bang* tour. It was a piece of expensive, sponsored, luxury action, at which the Stones had enveloped the stadium with irresistible nostalgic glory, with Keith Richards producing heroic conquistadorial riffs, and the brilliantly sybaritic Mick Jagger piloting his contortionist's torso through two untiring hours of horny, classic hits to justify the momentous ticket price. The 21st century Jagger phenomenon, half cartoon demon, half matey multi-millionaire, was an anorexic plutocrat, but still a confirmed hobo, with a mission to keep on rehabilitating the Stones through their creativity as Blues professionals to each new generation of disbelieving youth. And integrated into the drive-unit of their resiliently Rocky Blues, decorated now with baroque guitar tropes, there was the drummer Charlie Watts, still there as perennial time-warden, and as effortlessly sure of dictating the band's timing as though he was taking the Jag out for a spin in the country.

## DRIFT AWAY

It's like looking across a busy docks
a harbour industry to find the stage
remote as the modular ISS,
the band isolated as astronauts
doing moon-hops for mining platinum
ratcheting up a displaced 'Paint It Black'
or 'Midnight Rambler': do we note the clothes,
burgundy knee-length coats like highwaymen,
buccaneer boots: a time-slip seventies'
cryopreserved dressy unkillable
signature: low-slung belts accessorised
with Mexican skulls, Aztec turquoise lumps,
as though death's always a reality
closer than audience, randomised, curious
at physical resilience, the edge
just that much closer – guitar weaponry
the gunned offensive: do we see them now
as decommissioned celebs burning out
like redshift clusters, or still optimised
players in focus angled on runways
to do a solo; it's like a space-dock
the alienation, a blues band grouped there
meshing together as the world blows out.

## WHY THE ROLLING STONES ARE SO SKINNY

A neuroendocrine deficiency?
from circa 1963,
same body weight, same lasered to the bones
skinny confederacy:
average 63.5 kilograms
(140 pounds) topped by canned Guinness
as a black iron-compounded supplement
tasting of fermented Liffey.
Is it the light-speeding riffs keep them thin,
Chicago blues given amphetamine
guitar figures, or weird vasopressin
piloting the brain's chemistry?
Jagger's all carbohydrates: pasta, rice,
wholemeal bread, sushi for protein,
Richards and Woods spar cigarettes like chords,
nicotine-fencing and chase 'Nuclear' vodkas
slashed into orange (quadruples)
into liver toxicity,
streamlined defiance of all body laws,
a Stones individuated chemistry,
teeny bodies with reptilian pigment
like snakeskin grafted to anatomy.
Dysfunctional hypothalamus?
drugs or a Ferrari-charged stage anxiety,
they're wiry as contorted poppy stems
twisting their necks into dusty blue flower.
Their statement's irreversibly maintained,
skinnyness as salutary
the body copied like a guitar neck
and belted into max 30" jeans.
The riff for 'Jumpin' Jack Flash' strips off flesh
like meltdown, it's an aviation thrust
that shuts time down for the song's duration,
the licks so volatile, they're played on nerves
blasting a g-force assault on all calories.

# BANG

It's like a time-slip intervention:
a decommissioned plane
off-radar since 1978
arriving re-modified through blue fog
and catastrophic airways 2005
the Gulf offensive pathological genocide,
the psychotic bleed of twin oligarchs
absent from the frontline's blood reservoirs
big as Ontario – the Stones dust back
with edgy guitar brain-chatter, their war
a stripped compressed studio trio's focus
on shattering: energised torque and rip
rough as uncut diamonds refined
to black de-poshed hexagonal sparklers,
a re-bonded Jagger/Richards hands-on
mixture of diary and creative surge
like silver dazzle paint – two in a room –
start where they started, blues, 'Back of My Hand'
a Muddy Waters Little Walter rebrand
simplistic authenticity, first time
it's been disturbing combat raw
for thirty years – you hear it – 'Rough Justice'
or the coded Bush ode 'Sweet Neo Con'
mining the underbelly, but it's back
the blues apprentice facing down the times,
the disaffected greasing up the real.
'It's always scarlet, never pink or chartreuse'
Charlie complains, the mood-tempo, the feel
of music worked on under a car.
The sound's up, confrontational, the bang
a reworked restart from the blues kitchen
solid aggression like they're in your room
there with the sunset and the smoking bomb.

## LATER

Always later. DNA error
a mausoleum of guitar rejects
a red-tongued carbon footprint on the sky
hair-dye and reconstructed look
concision tight as levelling a gun
to end the final all
demented fatwah brains shattered against the wall.
*Voodoo Lounge* starts the later spooky tribe,
skull rings as hoodoo, printed pirate scarves,
Haiti occult amulets, a band
in which the driving music excludes death
as defensive offensive, do it loud
in a percussive circle, louder still
so later's safer and shatter 'Love Is Strong'
and maintain eponymous hierarchy
despite the vodka, fags, the Guinness cans,
customised drugs, zesty vintage champagnes,
the excess presidential lab, limos
bisecting concrete canyons. And later
it's dark in there, spacious as a hangar
and low-lit as a shatterproof
concrete bunker, the red exit sign blue,
the smell post-mortem, a post-gig vacuum
like makeup de-greased by a sponge later.
A dead Stone's like a rock pharaoh,
a jewelled alligator? Throw switches on
the stadium comes alive, the sound erupts,
the swooping buccaneers do two hours on
immersed in fandom, deferring later.

## BLACK AS A LIMO'S BLACK

It's where you hear it first – *A Bigger Bang*
like rocket re-entry – your global space –
physical location, the sound addressed
into you personally, like a new car's
military design theme, armoured panels,
high power rifle defeat and 'Rain Fall Down'
I got its time of life downturn integrated
at Cecil Court – a corridored alley
off Leicester Square, played loud in our bookshop's
subversive niche – one green light on titles
looking like submerged graffiti, the desk
a ruby slab on industrial fixtures.
We initialized *Bang* as shop soundtrack
a counterintuitive rock intelligence
on disruptive oil-guzzling in Iraq,
personal disintegration – face the wall
upwards of 50 and the bullets rain
until you fall. Sound scared up in the dark
'Look What The Cat Dragged In' and out again
into a full-on disordered reality.
*Bang*'s works destabilised the shop, kicked grooves
for purchase power, my local geography
of RS kick-back: rain inside, outside,
wiping all incidentals, diary stuff
from consciousness – the music in my veins
spooky as hoodies out in the back yard.

## SWAMP BLUES

A liver-toxic, muggy swamplands mix —
the Stones surfacing like alligators
to brew voodoo
soupy riffs in the studio.
Knobbled sexagenarian virtuosos

on skewed legs
socketed into chinos,
their sound's like ripped dark energy
accelerating from cosmic Big Bang
across a radiated universe,

mashed, sticky with its greenhouse scars
and manipulative oil wars.
They're like four figures turning gold
in a bunker urinal
a declassified rock hegemony,

no charts, just live
conquistadorial rock,
a global liquidation act,
extravagant funeral rites, light the fat
and keep on playing in the frying pan's

electrifying drizzle.
'Rough Justice' turns up like a bailiff's threat
throwing punches on the door.
A gritty street edge still skins their fingers
bleeding from abrasive chords

like stripping fish.
It's late, murky, a riffy cosh
of affirmative attitude
that they're invincible – bandit rockers,
skins printed out as dollars, cash,

wonky hats and leopard-print coats,
parading leather-baked longevity, dried out,
detoxed, gangsterish autocrats,
turning the volume up like overdose
or blow-out in a nose-up lifting jet.

## STONES 50

A turquoise drone, shimmying dragonfly
bullets a silver scratch on 1973
the time-slip retrieved by transitioning
youth as unimpeachable eye-shadow
smoky as LA fog, blue-strawberry,

I listened with LSD astronauts
to the first bootleg *Liver Than You'll Ever Be*
Oakland Colisseum 1969,
a licks-scorcher 'Carol' 'Little Queenie',
a driving lascivious muddy set

the sound come up in colours, orange, green,
saturated purple, already choice
providing a decade's lawless mood-board
like robbing banks, they get the hit and scram
and chase another in the getaway.

We floated, listening through bright gateways
above crystallized, then regrouping trees,
as though time separated from its speed.
An epoch crashed, the scrambled seventies
stood like a red guitar upright in sand.

Stones 50: it's like fifty studios,
each a guitar surgery left behind
with 30 songs, the mortality-trek
towards vanishing point – a bright red sun –
two drumsticks beating time on a coffin.

Stones 50: we're all waiting in the dark
for breaking news – death's a thing of the past –
the genes re-set, and looking for the band
to run on stage, are they renewed again
in spooky ways we'll never understand?